Praise for

# CRAFT YOUR OWN MAGIC

"In times that call us to be more present with the sacred, this book is a much-needed invitation. Craft Your Own Magic is a beautiful and comprehensive guide to deepening your connection with earth and spirit. Cassie's teachings are rooted in reciprocity, right relationship, and integrity. This book carries powerful embodied wisdom that I firmly believe has the capacity to change the world."

— **Asha Frost**, Indigenous medicine woman and author of
*You Are the Medicine*

"Craft Your Own Magic is a breath of fresh air for those of us feeling called to embrace our own unique kind of magic. Cassie shares generous guidance on forging an ethical, reciprocal path in a way that honors your imagination and celebrates the ever-evolving nature of magic. This book feels like sitting with a wise friend who empowers you to trust your intuition as you explore and create a personalized magical practice."

— **Edgar Fabián Frías**, artist, psychotherapist, educator, and brujx

"Cassie is a wealth of knowledge! I have read her books and interviewed her on my podcast, and her perspective is so refreshing in this industry. Cassie is able to break down spiritual concepts in such a tangible way and really respects the origins and the people from which these practices come. She has an innate wisdom that touches her reader and really helps them embody the earth's wisdom with universal love. Please buy anything this woman writes!"

— **Alea Lovely**, host of the *Spiritual Shit* podcast and author
of *Meaningful Manifestation*

# CRAFT YOUR OWN MAGIC

## ALSO BY CASSIE UHL

*Understanding the Wheel of the Year*

*Understanding Auras*

*Understanding Crystals*

*Understanding Chakras*

*Understanding Tarot*

*Journey Tarot*

*Soul Discovery Journal*

# CRAFT YOUR OWN MAGIC

Reawaken Your Intuition,
Understand Magical Correspondences, and
Create a Meaningful Personal Practice

## CASSIE UHL

**HAY HOUSE LLC**
Carlsbad, California • New York City
London • Sydney • New Delhi

**Cataloging-in-Publication is on file with the Library of Congress.**

**Tradepaper ISBN:** 978-1-4019-7523-4
**E-book ISBN:** 978-1-4019-7524-1
**Audiobook ISBN:** 978-1-4019-7525-8

10 9 8 7 6 5 4 3 2 1
1st edition, September 2024

Printed in the United States of America

This product uses responsibly sourced papers and/or recycled materials. For more information, see www.hayhouse.com.

Dedicated to the women who have carried, loved,
and inspired me:

my ancestral lineage of wise women;

my grandmothers, Carol and Eleanor;

my mother, Angela;

my sisters (bio and chosen);

my beloved mentors;

and the Great Mother.

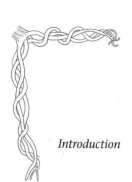

# CONTENTS

# INTRODUCTION

*"Everything moves, nothing stays or congeals long*
*enough to ever be fixed into being. Everything*
*is caught in the trance of becoming."*

— Dr. Báyò Akómoláfé, *These Wilds Beyond Our Fences*

Crafting your own magic is a process of remembering how to collaborate with the more-than-human and unseen realms as a co-conspirator in our collective evolution. It's a call to cultivate comfort amid the discomfort of crafting magic in the unknown. Throughout this book, I'll invite you to consider what a magical practice might look like for you without the aid of Internet searches and scripted spells. Where would you turn to seek inspiration, community, means, and modes to craft your magic? Perhaps you would shift inward to the trees, flowers, birds, or invisible in-between spaces. What crafting your own magic looks like for you will be personal and fluid. You won't find scripted spells and rituals within these pages. Instead, you'll find a collection of optional threads offering pathways to a magical practice rooted in your lived experience and the relationships you form in seen and unseen realms. Some of the threads in this book will speak to you more than others.

In crafting my own magic, I've learned to rely on trusting the intangible, free of labels and "correctness." I've also had to take a hard, honest look at my spiritual and magical journey and become aware of my Western urge to name and claim. I learned more about current systems of oppression that I both suffered under and of which I experienced the unearned benefits. Yet, these detours have also created openings to new pathways and a deeper connection with the animate world, spiritual realms, and myself. Eventually, these detours gave rise to a more radical and honest personal magical practice.

I hope that by sharing my uncertainty, messiness, thought processes, and real-time grappling with big questions, you are able to welcome the unknown and the mess as needed parts of your process too. It is from these places of discomfort, not knowing, and becoming that your magical practices can flourish.

You will notice that I address current systems of oppression throughout this book, such as colonialism, white supremacy, human supremacy, patriarchy, capitalism, etc.; there are others. I do not speak to these systems as an authority on them but express that becoming aware of them, unhooking from them, and making repairs (for some) have become an integral aspect of learning how to craft my own magic. While some might see these undercurrents as divisive, I have found them to be freeing. Regardless of your relationship status with these themes, I want to invite curiosity around how they can create pathways to a more honest and personal magical practice.

Your magical journey and practice will look different from mine and anyone else who reads this book. You will likely be taken off course, only to find that it was a necessary part of your unique journey. My goal is to offer you side posts along the way, whether you are on the trail or not. Simply put, what your spiritual and magical practices look like isn't something I can tell you, which is why you won't find doctrine or formulaic magic within this book. I will share techniques to hone your inherent intuitive abilities, personal experiences, and practices, all of which I will encourage you to modify to suit your needs. All the practices I offer are to assist you in better understanding your relationship with the energetic world, your environment, and your magical practice. This book is a call to rekindle *your* wisdom through *your* relationships with the seen and unseen realms you inhabit because they are your greatest teachers.

## Suggestions for Using This Book

You may have already discerned that this book is not a quick cure-all and does not follow a linear path. Crafting your own magic lives in the territory of becoming and emerging rather than knowing and finality. Some of the threads in this book will speak to you more than others, and some might make you angry or sad. I encourage you to incorporate the threads you feel you need while being cautious not to allow mild discomfort to keep you from weaving a more honest and reparative way of relating to your magical practice.

Because the foundation of crafting your own magic lives in respectful relationship building, slowness will inherently be part of it. Operating at a slower pace can be frustrating, especially when you feel like you're simultaneously healing and learning (or relearning) how to build a magical practice of your own. I understand deeply the desire to "arrive" at some undefinable truth or home. I'd be lying if I told you I always felt content with the pace of crafting my own magic. But I can tell you that the time I've poured into crafting my magical practice has been worth every moment and that, ironically, the more I discover what I don't know, the more grounded my practice feels.

Parts of this book might challenge you or require lengthy detours. If you need to put this book down for either reason, honor that. I trust you'll come back when and if you need or want to. I've found, in my practice, that anytime I wander off for a bit, the spirit realm is always excited to reconnect when I return.

I invite you to find a way to record your work throughout this book with the support of a journal, art-making, audio or video recording, or any other tool you feel called to work with as your practice expands. In some magical practices, this is called a grimoire, or a book of shadows. How you create a system to record your findings can be as unique as your practice. You may feel called to purchase particular magical tools at certain points. If you do, I encourage you to read Chapter 2 on ethics and ancestry before doing so.

Crafting your own magic is an invitation to sit in the unknown and befriend it. It is a slow and intentional dance between you, the living earth, and the energetic forces of the spirit realm. It lives in the past with your ancestors, your body, the land, the present moment, and the unfolding future.

Your magical practice and the path that shapes it will be as unique as you are, as it should be. When you pick up new threads, you might be taken in new directions far outside this book. In fact, I hope you are. Your unique vitality is needed, especially in the magical world. Learn from the past, but try not to cling to it. Listen to others, but try not to put them on a pedestal. Trust and honor the wisdom gained from the personal relationships you form with the animate and energetic world even when it seems foreign and unknown. Your unique flavor of magic is part of this rich, diverse, and mysterious web of life and holds an important role. It's time to pick up your sword of magic and wield it with care and courage.

CHAPTER 1

# WHAT IS CRAFTING YOUR OWN MAGIC?

*"Anybody depending on somebody else's gods is depending on a fox not to eat chickens."*

— Zora Neale Hurston, *Moses, Man of the Mountain*

rafting your own magic might sound like I'm asking you to make things up or not listen to others. I'm not. Crafting your own magic means you seek insight from others, both past and present, but with the aid of your intuition, discernment, and relationships with the more-than-human world and unseen realms. Throughout this book, you will be encouraged to trust and honor your inherent wisdom and insights you receive in relationship with your guides, spirits, the animate world, and local environment. Crafting magic in this may initially feel uncomfortable; it certainly did for me. The reality for most of us is that we've been living in systems where human supremacy and extraction have been normalized and examples of consensual and reciprocal relationships are sparse. Crafting magic from a lens of consensual and reciprocal relationship-building might initially feel strange, or nonintuitive, which is why your intuition cannot be the only source for a deeply rooted, sustainable, and reciprocal magical practice. Your intuition is fallible, or more accurately, your human interpretation of your intuition is fallible. This same line of thinking can be applied to our current understanding of the past, as interpreted by humans. My magical path has required me to be honest about our inherent imperfections as a species, and how to lean on my more-than-human relationships to cast a wider perspective.

Though this book won't focus on providing you with specific magical recipes or step-by-step spells, it will supply you with an abundance of guidance to create a magical practice of your own as well as structures to navigate possible confusion or discomfort you will likely encounter along the way. My hope is that this book will give you the necessary guidance, or where to seek it out from others, to feel secure in a personal magical practice informed by your uniquely lived experiences and relationships. It is imperative to note that crafting your own magic is *not* a free pass to steal and appropriate from other cultures, nor does it give you license to bestow yourself with titles from other cultures. We'll explore this more in Chapter 2. My magical practice has required deep nuance when it comes to understanding what crafting my own magic is—and is not—which I will address throughout these pages.

The truth is, a direct lineage to a magical or spiritual practice is quite rare for most of us. So many of us carry several ancestral lineages (some easier to track than others). Some reside on the same land as our ancestors, while many don't (some by choice, some by force), and nearly all of us have experienced some level of erasure (past and present) of our ancestors' spiritual and magical practices. Throughout this book, I will offer you ways to navigate having a limited connection to your magical lineage and how to craft your own magic regardless of your past. Working in this way allows you to create a unshakeable magical practice here, today, even if you're far from the people and land of your ancestors. I feel that this kind of magic is something many of us need permission to do right now. Part of crafting your own magic will include allowing yourself this permission.

Cancel culture has inserted a certain fear around how to proceed in magical and spiritual spaces. Rightfully so, as many white-bodied people, including me, have relied on cultural appropriation to mend our very real feelings of disconnection. This has in turn caused many to bypass opportunities to heal our personal wounds around colonization and erasure. Not only is this harmful to the historically marginalized communities facing colonization and erasure today, but it's a mere Band-Aid for our wounds. Though crafting one's own magic can easily be done free of cultural appropriation, it will not absolve those who need to make repairs. I think these issues have left many of us with a feeling of tiptoeing around our magical practices, wondering where to turn or from whom to learn, which has had the unintended effect of stripping us of our innate magical abilities. Crafting your own magic is a permission slip to create a deeply personal and powerful magical practice regardless of where you live and from where you came. Of course, there will be nuance for each of us, depending on where you live, your lived experience, and your ancestry.

My story may or may not resonate with yours, but I suspect aspects of it will ring true. As a European American living on stolen land, I hold various Northern and Central European ancestries, primarily from England, Germanic countries, Sweden, Denmark, and Scotland. My grandmother emigrated from England to the United States while pregnant with my father. Though I am grateful for such a close emotional and historical connection to my ancestral lands of England, the physical distance between my ancestral lands and where I live today creates a vast chasm of disconnection. Beyond my disconnection from the land my ancestors came from, there were generations of erasure, oppression, and violence that my ancestors endured as Christianity spread. Being born and raised in America, I have to approach my magical practice from my ancestry as an outsider, which requires a special kind of nuance and care so that I do not appropriate from or cause harm to the very people I came from.

On the other hand, my relation to the land I'm on in America is fraught due to being a European settler. I reside on stolen land. Entire ecosystems and the Indigenous peoples who tended this land for thousands of years experienced violence, death, forced assimilation, and erasure at the hands of my ancestors and continue to face injustice today. When I form relationships with the land I live on today, I must consider the brutal history my ancestors inflicted on the land and the Native people, and how those harms continue to this day. I will not be able to form meaningful relationships with the land and its inhabitants if I am not willing and able to feel the discomfort of this harm and actively make repairs. For these reasons, crafting your own magic will undoubtedly look different for all. Someone of African or South American descent would have a vastly different set of steps to craft their own magic here in the United States, than would someone living in Australia or Canada.

Understanding your unique ancestry and relationship to the land you live on will be an intrinsic part of crafting your own magic and something I will not shy away from here. Furthermore, the unlearning and repairs that may need to happen to connect you more deeply with your magical practice, depending on your unique ancestral lineages, is something I cannot do for you. You might also have deep and current wounds to tend to. I have included a resource section in the back of this book that offers support or unlearning for Black, Brown, Indigenous, and white-bodied folks from various healers and teachers I've worked with along my journey of crafting my own magic.

## Defining Magic and Other Helpful Terms

I chose to use the word *magic* in this book because I find it to be more flexible than other words like *spellwork* or *witchcraft*. You'll notice I still use these words, because we have a long and winding past with them. But for the purpose of this book, I will primarily use the words *magic*, *magical practice*, and *magical workings* to describe the essence of this book and its offerings. Regardless of where your ancestors came from, where you came from, or where you live now, you can craft magic.

We all have access to magic, and I will encourage you throughout this book to determine what magic looks and feels like for you. To build a common language, I will offer you my definition of *magic*, which is an inherent ability to intentionally shift energy to create emotional, spiritual, and physical change through cooperative reciprocation. Borrow it if you need it, but I hope that throughout this book, you will come up with a definition that feels resonant to you. Let's explore the last part of my definition of *magic*—"cooperative reciprocation"—as I feel like it is the point where this book may break from others. If you believe that all beings—human, plant, animal, or otherwise—are living and as a result are inherently sovereign, we must assume that we cannot force a being to do our bidding, magic or otherwise. This, in my opinion, is why spells and magic sometimes fall flat, cause harm, or don't produce desired outcomes. For example, I'm guessing that you would never walk up to a stranger and ask them to help you manifest a new job or heal your childhood traumas. You would likely get to know them first, make sure you're a good fit to work together, and get their consent to help you. Yet most of us have been taught to conduct our magic without building a relationship with or gaining consent from the spirits and energies we employ or call upon.

In crafting my own magic, I've learned that for my magic to be effective and not harmful, it needs to be rooted in relationship and reciprocity. What I mean by this is that I do not flippantly use mugwort in a spell; rather I connect with the spirit of mugwort to ask if it would like to assist me in my magic, and I work with it collaboratively. These ideas are not new. Indigenous healers, medicine people, wise women, shamans, druids, witches, and countless others have practiced in this way, have known this from the beginning, and continue to practice in these ways today. The erasure of our magical practices varies, but we were all Indigenous at some time, and many spiritual and magical practices were and still are rooted in relationship and reciprocity. We'll explore this in greater depth in Chapter 3.

In some circles, you may see the word *magick* used. I use this word sometimes too. The word *magick* was coined by Aleister Crowley in the early 1900s.[1] Aleister Crowley has been influential in various magical circles but is hardly representative of all magical practices. For this reason, I find it important to use the word *magic*. Some relate magic without the "*k*" to a magician pulling a rabbit out of a hat, which was one reason why Crowley preferred the word *magick*. I don't find this correlation between a magical performance and a magical practice inherently bad. For outsiders without a magical practice, watching your magic-making may very well seem like you're pulling metaphorical rabbits out of hats with the changes you create, and that's not a bad thing. Ultimately, I am making a case for an all-encompassing and more accessible word that represents the art of intentionally shifting and changing energy regardless of how you identify your craft. Right now, *magic* fits the bill. Of course, if you already have a relationship with a word that better describes what I've outlined as "magic," by all means, use that.

An exploration of synonyms for the word *magic* may help you find ways to define *magic* for yourself. Here's a list of synonyms for the word *magic* from Thesaurus.com: *alchemy, wizardry, power, incantation, conjuring, spell, prophecy, enchantment, divination, sooth-saying, witchcraft, voodoo, illusion, occultism.* As you can see, there are words in this list that span various cultures, reiterating the fact that we all hold magic. I find the word *power* to be the most interesting word on this list. Shifting and molding energy is indeed powerful. The erasure and dismissal of magical practices world-wide have affected us to different degrees, often with the intent to cut us off from our power. The endless vending machine of online spells and rituals can make it feel like magic is a simple copy-and-paste act. You're not alone if you find yourself grasping for truth and a deeper sense of power in your magical practices.

There are many other words that I'll use throughout this book that will be helpful in establishing some common ground. Due to the English language being somewhat limiting, I find that some-times there's confusion around these words, or differences in opin-ion, which is also valid. Though most of the definitions are commonly agreed upon, you might not agree with all of my defi-nitions and that's okay. What's important is that you understand what I mean when I say them in this book, but you need not adopt my meanings of them.

- **Animism** – The belief that everything, including, plants, animals, stones, houses, and all other seemingly "inanimate" objects are alive and sovereign, to varying degrees. Acknowledging the animate world is a common thread that weaves throughout many magical and spiritual practices the world over and is a belief held by many Indigenous cultures. Animism is a complex word that means different things to different cultures and practitioners.

- **Energy** – The intangible essence that exudes from both the physical or seen world and nonphysical or unseen realms—e.g., the energy contained in a physical tree versus an unseen spirit guide. Both physical and nonphysical beings contain and exude energy. Though the word *energy* can be used interchangeably with the word *spirit* at times, in my practice, it is not always interchangeable, which is why I tend to use the word *energy*. For example, if I collect a branch from a tree, the spirit of that tree will still be with the tree; however, some of its energy or essence will be contained in the branch. Similarly, your soul or spirit does not leave you when you shed dead skin or hair, yet your energy will still be imprinted on them.

- **Intuitive Severance** – Moments within your ancestry or your current lived experience when you or your ancestors were severed from your magical and spiritual practices due to oppression, colonization, religious persecution, or violence. Intuitive severances can occur to all people regardless of race, gender, or ancestry. They may occur by choice, out of self-preservation, or by force.

- **Mundane World or Ordinary Reality** – Each of these words describes the physical or seen world and can be used interchangeably. Keep in mind, these words are not meant to exist as a binary. Sometimes the lines between ordinary reality (or the mundane world) and non-ordinary reality (or the otherworld) and the things we do in them can blur! Two examples of this might include being hit with a wave of intuitive information while grocery shopping, or noticing a hawk while driving and intuitively knowing that it carries a message for you.

- **Otherworld or Non-ordinary Reality** – These words describe the unseen or nonphysical realms we engage with, intentionally or unintentionally. They can also be used interchangeably. Usually, engaging with non-ordinary reality or otherworld requires some effort, but not always! Some examples of intentionally engaging with non-ordinary realities are embarking on an otherworld journey, astral travel, giving or receiving energy healing, channeling, shape-shifting, and exploring the dreamworld.

- **Ritual** – These are regular, sometimes daily or seasonal actions that you take to complete a certain task or to create a specific outcome. Rituals can involve or take place in ordinary reality, non-ordinary reality, or both. Brushing your teeth every day is an example of a mundane ritual, whereas giving daily offerings to your guides and allies might be viewed as a ritual that is more otherworldly in nature. Other magical rituals might include cleansing your energy, updating your altar(s) for different seasons or celebrations, or harvesting specific plants in specific ways at specific times. Similar to spells, rituals are often performed to shift or change energy, but not always. There is overlap between spells and rituals, but they are not always the same.

- **Spell** – Spells comprise a set of actions with a defined beginning and ending intended to create a specific change or outcome. Spells can be simple or complex and vary vastly from practitioner to practitioner. Lighting a candle for protection is a spell, and dancing under a full moon in Sagittarius on a Thursday to connect with your ancestors is a spell. They each have a defined beginning, ending, set of actions, and a desired outcome. I use the word *spell* to describe a unique process that may not be repeated, and I use the word *ritual* to describe a process that will be repeated regularly. The intentions behind the two often, but not always, differ. Rituals create a continuous flow of energy in the same direction, whereas spells orient energy more directly and intermittently. Unlike rituals, a spell might only happen once, by choice or because it's impossible. But if you repeat a spell regularly, it can *become* a ritual. Rituals can be spells, but spells are not always rituals. An example of a spell that is also a ritual might be saying a specific phrase or incantation over your water before ingesting it. In this situation, the spell is the spoken incantation directing specific energy into the water a single time or intermittently for a defined purpose. It becomes a ritual if you repeat these actions regularly, directing a continuous energy flow toward the water for a specific purpose.

- **Spirit Allies** – Spirit allies, like energy, cross the threshold between ordinary and non-ordinary reality. Circling back to animism, many people—myself included—believe that humans as well as the more-than-human world (plants, stones, land, etc.) have spirits. However, spirits do not require a physical container. There are many spirits, ancestors, guides, etc., who exist solely in non-ordinary reality. I liken spirits to the fullest expression of a being, whether it has a physical container or not, and where its energy can be expressed and sensed in various ways. For example, a tree spirit can contain the energy of the element of water without being a water spirit.

Some of these words mean very different things to different people, even within magical and spiritual spaces. Spirit and ritual are commonly used in many organized religions, which can make defining them even more confusing. As you can see, when we start to really dig in to possible meanings for these words, there's quite a bit of nuance and variety. Along with the suppression of magic, the vocabulary to describe it has also been suppressed. Language is constantly in flux, but some limitations around describing and discussing magic are intentional, so explaining what I mean when I use specific words is essential. You are not only reclaiming your magical practice, you're also reclaiming how you communicate about it.

## The Five Elements of Crafting Your Own Magic

The threads needed to craft your own magic will be presented through the lens of the elements: earth, air, fire, water, and Spirit. There are references to four or five elements in spiritual and magical practice worldwide, and they've become a cornerstone of my practice. The accessibility and pervasiveness of the elements lend themselves to being an ideal foundation for crafting your own magic. Each area of crafting your own magic is paired with one of these five elements, allowing you to passively engage with each element simply by reading this book. This will not be the entirety of your relationship with each element, but my desire is that it will give you a solid foundation if you are new to them.

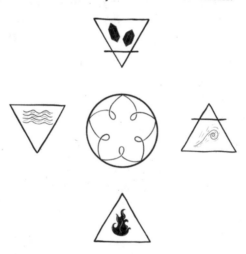

These are the five elements of crafting your own magic:

1. AIR – Intuition
2. FIRE – Relationship
3. WATER – Correspondences
4. EARTH – Ethics and Ancestry
5. SPIRIT – Crafting Your Magic

In cyclically shifting from one element to the other, these five guideposts have helped create an unshakeable foundation for my magical practice.

We'll begin with the element of earth, where you'll be encouraged to connect with your ancestors and build an ethical framework to ensure your magical path includes care and respect for all life. Next you'll move into the element of air, where you'll learn ways to deepen your relationship with your unique intuitive abilities. From there, we'll circle to the element of fire, where you'll begin forming relationships with the energetic and spiritual world around you. As you spiral to the element of water, you'll be encouraged to understand how those relationships correspond with each other and how they can be worked with in your magical practice. Finally, you'll begin crafting your own magic for the element of Spirit.

I liken the elements to a bridge between the magical world and the mundane world. They are the wordless and infinite energies that shape everything we experience and can help us better organize and assign meaning to our magical experiences in the physical world. Though they can be touched or felt physically—you can touch the earth, feel the wind—their energy extends far beyond the physical world. They will be a thread that weaves throughout this book and, hopefully, your spirit as you craft your own magic.

Throughout each element, I'll share some of the ways I've crafted a meaningful, magical practice and offer you exercises to do the same. Nothing I share is with the intention that you will take the same path I did. Rather, I will offer customizable tools and exercises so you can craft a magical practice that feels the most aligned and doable for you, in your current season.

## The "Witch" Label and Identity

We humans love labels. If you're reading this book, I bet that having a title or a label for your spiritual path is something you've thought about and perhaps even struggled with. Throughout my spiritual and magical practice, I spent years seeking a title that felt like my own. From Buddhist, Yogini, to witch. None of them fit, sometimes because they were rooted in cultural appropriation, sometimes because they just didn't feel true for me. I've learned to accept this and am content with the possibility that there may not be a single word to express my relationship with my magical and spiritual practice. Colonization, religious persecution, and erasure have stripped this away from many of us. The upside to not having the words to label myself or the ability to access much written information about my ancestors' magical practices is that I've learned to trust my internal wisdom keepers, guides, intuition, and ancestors. You, too, might arrive at a place where you find living in these unknown and unnamable territories a beautiful place to be.

I bring this up because, to some, what I share in this book might seem to be witchcraft. The truth is, it is and it isn't. I suspect there might be someone reading this who, like me, never really resonated with the title "witch." Even though many people associate magic, ritual, and spellwork with the realm of the witch, *you do not have to be a witch to practice any of these things.* One of my goals in this book is to öffer you an alternative to the narrative that practicing magic means you're a witch. It means so many different things for different people and has meant different things throughout history. The title "witch" is extremely broad and rarely honors our complex and winding ancestries; in some ways, it even perpetuates the erasure of ancestral wisdom and language. In other ways, the word *witch* has become exclusionary. Witches are often stereotyped as women, yet throughout history, all gender expressions have practiced various forms of sorcery, healing, and magic.

Because *witch* is such a loaded word, I want to spend some time sitting with it. Perhaps you already identify as a witch. If so, that's great. Maybe you're on the fence, or perhaps it's a word that makes you feel uncomfortable. This is also wonderful. What you call yourself is not for me to say. You might have a beautiful relationship with the word *witch* and feel like it's a powerful reclamation. If this is you, claim it with pride! For others, it might feel inauthentic, or it might feel like a derogatory label. Though I do use the words *witch* and *witchcraft* at times to explain my practice more easily, they are not titles or labels that I prefer to claim. You might not either, and that's okay. There's a rich history of beautiful regional labels and titles to describe various magical and spiritual practices across the world. Now, claiming or using these more specific and regional titles might not be accessible for other reasons, such as cultural appropriation, which we'll get to later, but I think they're important to know about. You might find learning about them deeply healing.

Living in this dominant culture that relishes labeling, not having one can add a layer of pain and a sense of not being enough. The origins of the word *witch* are debated, but many believe it may originate from the Old English *wicce*. *Wicce* once meant "female magician, sorceress," but was later used to suggest "a woman supposed to have dealings with the devil or evil spirits."[2] As you can see, *witch* is a tricky word! To give you a taste of just how varied our language has been, and still is in some places, to describe magical folk here are some examples, in Spanish, *curandero* means "healer"[3]; the English phrase "cunning woman" refers to a "wisewoman"[4]; in Zulu, *isángoma* translates to "diviner"[5]; the Old Irish word *fáidh* translates to "prophet"[6]; in Croatian, *vilenica* translates to "faery-woman"[7]; and in Sámi, *rudok* means "spokeswoman for the female supernatural"[8] (my favorite).

There are specific and intentional words associated with various modes of magic, healing, and divination in nearly all our heritages. You do not have to be a witch, have witches in your lineage, or identify with the word *witch* to tap into your inherent magical abilities. We all carry magic within our blood, bones, and ancestors, even if you do not have a label to claim. If you do decide to identify yourself and your practice with some sort of label, I hope you take the time to sit with the words you choose. Remember, your words have power. Words are spells.

If you're reading this, but you don't claim the label of "witch," you likely still have the sort of internal wound commonly referred to as the "witch wound" in many magical spaces. I think we all do. I refer to this internal wound as an intuitive severance. Intuitive severances are points within your physical ancestry when ancestors either chose or were forced to stop using their intuition and magical practices due to religious persecution, colonization, or violence. Common practices many of our ancestors may have been forced to stop or hide include energetic healing, herbalism, spellwork, ancestor reverence, Goddess worship, collaboration with spirits, and oracular abilities, to name a few. The moments within your ancestry when people were forced to hide these abilities or stop practicing them can create a severance between you and how your ancestors once practiced magic. Mending these intuitive severances can be vital in reclaiming a magical practice that feels true deep in your bones. We will explore intuitive severances in-depth in Chapter 3.

## Uprooting Patriarchy

You may find that tending to intuitive severances sometimes opens painful doors that lead to identifying, addressing, and uprooting patriarchy from within yourself and your ancestral line. When patriarchy is the sea in which most of us swim, it's only natural that it would influence our magical practices; this goes for everyone, as patriarchy harms us all, even (especially) men. A simple definition of *patriarchy* is "a society where men hold most of the power." Patriarchy is by no means the only system of oppression that many of us live within. Racism, colonialism, ableism, ageism, capitalism, and classism can each have an impact on your magical practice, and it's important to be aware of them. As a European American woman, I will speak primarily to patriarchy, as it is the oppressive system with which I am most intimately familiar.

Let's start by looking at an example about Gerald Gardner. He is often touted as the father of modern witchcraft and is one of the founders of the religion of Wicca. This illustrates one of the many ways our current relationship with magic and witchcraft has been influenced by patriarchy. Wicca is often lumped together with witchcraft as being one and the same, but it is not. Witchcraft is an umbrella term that contains many nonreligious spiritual and magical practices. Yet, Wicca has had a far-reaching influence on modern-day magic, so much so that many do not realize that witchcraft is not synonymous with Wicca and that many of Wicca's tenets—such as the emphasis on "the rule of three"—do not pertain to all who practice magic and witchcraft.

In Gemma Gary's book *Silent as the Trees: Devonshire Witchcraft, Folklore and Magic*, she outlines the relationship between Gerald Gardner and a Cunning magic practitioner named Cecil Williamson. I believe their relationship represents an important example of one way in which magical practices with roots in Europe have split from magic rooted in more matrilineal themes of relationship. According to Gary, Cecil, who learned primarily from local wise women practicing Cunning folk magic, "held firmly to the opinion that one could not work effective witchcraft without first attaining a working relationship with a familiar spirit." She goes on to share that "Cecil writes of his surprise and frustration that Gerald Gardner showed no interest in the concept of the familiar spirit, despite its central position within the lore of British witchcraft and folk magic, and it remains curiously absent within the established traditions of Wicca." Wicca has undeniably continued to have a tremendous impact on how many people practice magic today. Yet, the relational aspects of the regional folk magic were left out because Gerald Gardner was "really rather afraid of the whole idea of spirits," according to Gary.

If you're a fan of Wicca or the Golden Dawn (the Golden Dawn heavily influenced Wicca) hear me out. I do not share this to say that Wicca or the influences of the Golden Dawn on Wicca are wrong, only that some rather important pieces were left out. Because Wicca and Gardner have had such an impact on modern-day witchcraft, it would behoove us to recognize that dominant narratives around spellwork and magic have omitted the idea of forming relationships with the animate world and spirits. I wish I'd learned sooner that my magic would be more nourishing, communal, and powerful had I initially approached it through a lens of forming relationships rather than memorizing tables and charts of correspondences. This example is one of many that illustrates how patriarchy has influenced our magical practices; there are, unfortunately, many more that span across cultures.

Patriarchal influences may be far-reaching in your practice. Every time I come to a new phase in my magical practice, I tend to find new opportunities to address and heal the influences of patriarchy and other oppressive systems within myself and my magical practice. Here are other ways you might see it show up:

- Rejecting intuitive insights because you're not sure if they're true

- Relying on others to tell you how to craft your magic

- Opting for individualism over community in your magical practice (in both seen and unseen realms)

- Being ashamed of or hiding your magical practice or intuitive abilities

- Doubting the power of your magical skills

- Believing that crafting magic is only about getting what you want

- Being afraid to stand up for beliefs supported by your magical and spiritual practice, such as the well-being of plants, animals, all people, and the earth

It's important to note that these examples can result from various forms of oppression not limited to patriarchy and will vary in severity from person to person due to other systems of oppression. Understanding the nuance of intersectionality, a term created by Kimberlé Crenshaw,[9] as it pertains to patriarchy is important. Neglecting intersectionality can lead to "white feminism," or feminism that ignores white privilege.[10] Exploring the nuance of intersectionality and white feminism is outside this book's scope and my education. Still, it is important to understand, even in your magical practice, especially if you are of European descent and white. You might find that crafting your own magic is more about uprooting and unlearning rather than gaining and acquiring. Sometimes, when the harmful narratives that don't belong are healed and cleared, you'll find a pathway for your magic to come through. Much of crafting my own magic has involved learning how to uproot patriarchy from me and my practice so I can reconnect with the precolonial and pre-patriarchal wise ancestors within my lineage. It has also enabled me to craft a magical practice that is more cyclical in nature.

## Restoring Cyclical Magic

 Our bodies, like the earth, move in regenerative cycles of birth, growth, descent, death, and rebirth. Yet, in much of the modern world these regenerative cycles are controlled, feared, and demonized. Disdain for cycles abound and can be seen in desires to control the more-than-human world, laws that prohibit women and birthing bodies from body autonomy, the cultural pressure to avoid evidence of aging, discomfort and denial around death, obsessions with purity and cleanliness, and the erasure of Goddess and earth-based beliefs. Yet, for most of our human past these innately magical cycles have been celebrated, honored, and revered. Many magical practices, cross-culturally, were matrilineal, meaning they honored maternal bloodlines in reverence of the regenerative cycles displayed in womb bearers and women. Restoring cyclical magic does not mean being anti-men or wanting domination over men. Instead, it is a call to restore balance in a world that is so obviously out of balance with the innate and natural cycles of our bodies and the natural world.

When you begin working more cyclically in your magical practice, you will likely find, by default, that you become more relational and communal. Patriarchal expressions tend to favor competition and dominance, whereas the feminine tends to favor relationships and community. Competition and dominance are not inherently bad, but when their balancing force (the relational, communal, cyclical, etc.) has been obfuscated, they can quickly turn violent. I share the previous statements through a lens of gender fluidity, meaning that men, women, nonbinary people, and trans people can each hold varying degrees of these different expression. I also want to recognize that the words *masculine* and *feminine* might not resonate with you. They are words that I work with in my practice and will use occasionally throughout this book, but it is perfectly acceptable to replace them with something that feels more aligned with you and your practice. One option is to replace masculine with outward-flowing energy or force and feminine with inward-flowing energy or force. Or, perhaps plants, animals, deities, or elements embody these expressions that could be suitable replacements in your practice. Be creative; this is your practice!

The relational and communal aspects of crafting magic are rooted deeply in working more cyclically. The earth and the moon, commonly associated with the Goddess, steadily cycle through curiosity, expansion, contraction, death, and rebirth phases. Yet, these phases do not happen in isolation; they require relationships with other beings and forces to continue their cycles. The moon requires the sun's light and the earth's movement to move into a new phase each night. Our earth is a web of relationships between the blowing wind, transformative fire, shape-shifting water, and regenerative soil.

The magical qualities of moving through life more cyclically have been severely stifled and often replaced with linearity since patriarchy became the dominant narrative. This deficit has had an impact on our everyday lives and magical practices. I will share approaches and alternatives to dominant magical narratives throughout this book to help mend patriarchal wounds, which will help you reweave a more relational, cyclical, and communal magical practice.

The truth is, we humans have spent much more of our past, the world over, honoring and celebrating the Goddess and her generative aspects than we have living within the confines of patriarchy. In her book *The Flowering Wand: Rewilding the Sacred Masculine*, Sophie Strand speaks to this when she writes, "Tarot cards, astrology, psychism, herbalism, and body work are typically viewed as 'soft' or feminine. The dominant culture characterizes these practices as silly. But it is important to remember that this is only because the centuries-long Inquisition managed to eradicate whole populations of alternative healers and intuitive. It's easier to make fun of witches when all of the witches are dead."

The pentagram of Venus—the design on the cover and throughout this book—results from an 8-year cycle of the orbit of Venus viewed from Earth.[11] (Find the link to watch an animated video of the 8-year cycle in the notes section of this book; it's incredible!) The symbol exists due to a relational dance between Earth, the sun, and Venus. Venus is an ancient Latin Goddess associated with themes of cultivation, regeneration, and, later, love and beauty. As many realize a need to reintegrate themes related to a communal and generative Earth Goddess, it seems a fitting symbol to connect with in this book. Traditional pentagrams have been utilized by religious, spiritual, and occult practices for thousands of years. Yet, it feels important to work with a symbol that honors the relational, communal, and generative themes the pentagram of Venus displays.

Due to our collective amnesia around accessing and utilizing intuition, magic, and healing modalities, you may find acquiring relational and cyclical magic sources from your ancestry difficult. If you feel like this, you are not alone. My deepest desire is that the words, imagery, and invitations within this book serve as a healing salve and compass, enabling you to reclaim the once prominent relational, communal, and cyclical magical practices that are alive and well in your body, the earth, and the cosmos. If you work with the traditional pentagram, maybe, like me, you'll feel a pull to lean in to the pentagram of Venus throughout this book.

## Magic That Transcends Timelines

There is certainly value in looking to the past, and I will encourage you to do so for specific purposes but not to inform the entirety of your magical practice. Most cultures have endured a certain level of erasure or have had their spiritual practices rewritten by people outside of the original culture. In my ancestry, rooted in various countries throughout Northern Europe, most of the original magical practices were passed down orally. When they were recorded, Christian monks often observed the practices from the outside. This is not an uncommon story for magical and spiritual practices in other cultures too. For these reasons, it's my opinion that while it's important to understand the magical history of your ancestors, doing so through a lens of curiosity rather than fact can be liberating.

I have found far more depth and meaning in crafting a personal practice that combines written history, personal intuitive insights, relationship-building with my local environment (mundane and magical), ancestral connections, and the wisdom of others. Approaching your magical practice this way will often be more time consuming and require deeper trust in your intuitive abilities. It also requires deep awareness and allowance for nuance. I've found relying solely on history or the experiences of others as a foundation for my magical practice creates far too many opportunities to let patriarchy, white supremacy, and colonialism dictate my magic. In discussing relationship with the past, philosopher Báyò Akómoláfé cautions "sometimes in our quest to go back, we actually re-entrench, or reinforce and reinscribe the modern. It's the deeply modern way of thinking to situate time on a simple linearity and to conveniently locate the Indigenous in an originary Puritan past that can be resuscitated by some kind of advocacy, conservationism, preservationism, or reconstructionism. I feel that the Indigenous is melting and moving and traveling and migrating; that the modern, too, is a form of Indigeneity, and it too is traveling. And that we cannot easily parse or divide the world between "we're in an evil world right now and once it was good and fine and dandy," so that our work is much more complex. It's about listening, more than just restoring an image."[12]

In some spiritual and magical spaces, there's a fetishization of the past that, I believe, has the potential to distract from what the present is inviting. I will encourage you throughout this book to be aware of the ways linearity and binary ways of thinking might be distracting you from broader possibilities. This is not a call to neglect or ignore our available history, but it is an invitation to be aware of how much it's influencing your magical practice.

While you need not feel bound by the history available about your ancestors, it can be valuable and informative to develop a present-day relationship with them. I will provide practices within this book to connect with your ancestors, whether you know who they are or not. The relationships you form with your ancestors today do not need to be informed by what you know about them and their stories, but they can be. When you approach life knowing that all is magic and all is energy—which transcends time—the connections to your past can never be severed. Your ancestors' wisdom is alive and real today and lives within the earth, and your blood and bones.

Another aspect you may have personally experienced or witnessed is following the doctrine of present-day spiritual teachers without adequate reflection or discernment. Like our past, the present has been influenced by various belief systems, ranging from healing to deadly. There are undeniable oppressive systems woven throughout all our experiences to varying degrees. As you approach magical and spiritual practices from present-day teachers, it's important that, just as in exploring history, you do so with discernment—including while reading this book.

Either side of the binary, relying purely on the past or the present, strips away your autonomy, relational wisdom, personal gnosis, and the endless potential found in the present moment.

If you're wondering where that leaves you and your magical practice, don't worry—it's where all the most exciting and fulfilling magic lives, in the emerging unknown. This is where you'll be required to think for yourself and become open to endless possibilities. A practice informed by your relationships and experiences does not mean you cannot look to the past or learn from others. Not at all. I do both and will encourage you to do both. However, I will invite you to be intentional and discerning when you do. Crafting my own magical practice has taught me how to get comfortable in uncomfortable spaces. I've learned how to be okay with not having all the answers exactly when I want them and have become better at trusting my experiences even when I can't prove their existence by rational standards.

I spent much of my young adult life trying to find my "spiritual home" in borrowed or appropriated practices, by clinging to the past, or by extracting other people's truths. None of these approaches felt like home; some caused harm, requiring repair. I reached a point in my practice when all the places I used to look to find my answers disappeared or no longer rang true, or I discovered how harmful they were—coming to this place forced me to turn to my immediate surroundings, go inward, and excavate deeper trust in my intuitive connections. I found my spiritual home and most powerful magical practice when I threw out the binary of solely clinging to the past or relying on others to inform my practice. I began forming relationships directly with the mundane and magical within my local environment, my ancestors, and the spirit realm, through a personal lens.

Your spiritual path and ancestry may hold a nuanced variety of erasure, pain, joy, deep connection, and magic. If you have ever felt displaced, like you don't belong, or don't have a spiritual practice of your own, this book is for you. It is for the spiritual misfits, the ones who welcome the mystery and aim to find peace in the not-knowing. Even if it makes no sense within the comfortable confines of the recorded past, if you are bold you can create a practice that feels true to you. This is the book I wish I had when I was a young girl eager for depth, meaning, and magic in a confusing world that, in many ways, was set up to keep me from my own magic. This book is an invitation to craft your own magic.

Crafting your own magical practices doesn't mean you need to disconnect from everything you've learned and start over from scratch. But sometimes it might feel like you're starting over, especially for those who, like me, leaned in to cultural appropriation to find meaning. Your winding path has wisdom to give you, even the confusing and hard parts. There might be times when you feel overwhelmed with shame and want to quit or completely disconnect from your past. These themes have certainly been a part of my path.

Your ability to change and transform your magical practice over time is powerful and has the potential to bring a lot of healing to the world. The internal calls to shed and transform parts of your practice may come more frequently as your magical practices deepen. There will likely be parts of your practice that need to die away completely as you grow. These deaths can sometimes be painful, even life-altering, but they also create the rich compost that will inevitably feed your unique story and magical path. When you enter an underworld phase while crafting your own magic, I invite you to remember that, like the moon's changing appearances, it is just a phase. You will not stay there forever.

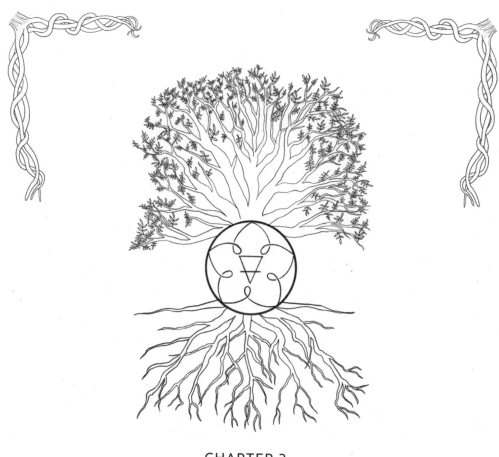

CHAPTER 2

# EARTH:
## ETHICS AND
## ANCESTRY

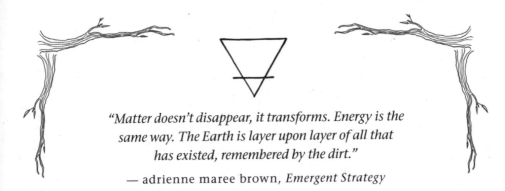

*"Matter doesn't disappear, it transforms. Energy is the same way. The Earth is layer upon layer of all that has existed, remembered by the dirt."*

— adrienne maree brown, *Emergent Strategy*

It would be difficult to discuss any magical practice without stepping into the realms of ethics and ancestry. Most magic practitioners are no strangers to the world of ethics, and if you're not, welcome! This world needs your practice to be deeply rooted in a consciously crafted ethical framework. Ethics and magic go hand in hand because magic is real and effective. To be able to regularly run your magical workings through a consciously crafted ethical framework is a practice in harm reduction. No amount of ethics will prevent you from never causing harm. You are human. However, having a keen awareness of your ethics will give you the necessary tools to repair those harms, do better in the future, and help steer your magical compass. Understanding your unique ancestral lineages will be a big part of building your ethical framework.

As we navigate this nuanced and sometimes rocky terrain of ethics and ancestry, we will do so with the support and strength of the element of earth. In several practices, including mine, the North is associated with the element of earth and wintertime. It is the realm of death and rebirth; these are two sides of the same coin that cannot be separated. In the heart of winter, the earth appears to be at rest, but within the soil, a slow and steady decomposition and integration is happening. The groundwork is being prepared for the eventual rebirth of spring. Within the cauldron of the North, winter, and the element of earth, we find wisdom and ways to begin assimilating information to lay the proper groundwork for an ethical framework. As your awareness grows around your ancestry and place in this world, you may find yourself in a position where you need to find stillness to integrate information on a deeper level. In doing so, you might find that some parts of your practice no longer fit and may need to die away to make room for new structures. There is no end to an ethical framework—like life and the entirety of your magical practice, it will always be an evolving part of your craft. Wintertime is a season that will come around again and again, and in this same vein, you will be given opportunities to examine and restructure your magical ethical framework. Each time you do, like the alchemy of the earth in winter, you will be held and supported within this same inner cauldron to incorporate ethics that guide your work.

The North and element of Earth are also the home of the ancestors in many practices. In a very physical way, the earth holds the wisdom of your ancestors. The blood and bones of all those who've come before you, human and more-than-human, are part of the soil. You are made of this same earth and, therefore, in many ways, so are your ancestors. Beyond our connection to the earth, the study of epigenetics continues to show us how the behaviors and environments of our ancestors can affect us today.[1] Similar to your ethics, creating a relationship with your ancestry will be an important part of crafting magic that will also inform your ethical framework. Ethics and ancestry are deeply intertwined and can help guide you in your ever-evolving magical practice. As with ethics, building a relationship with your ancestry is individual. Within each person's ancestry lives a vastness of rich storytelling, grief, joy, sadness, and magic. Yet, not all will have access to this information. We each carry various levels of separation from our ancestors for many reasons. Though I will not have all the answers for you, we will explore ethics and ancestry through various lenses and with the support of leaders in the field.

Real and sometimes painful barriers keep many of us from knowing our ancestors and their practices. Some are more present than others. I have found great importance in understanding the nuance of both the harm caused to my ancestors and the harm my ancestors have caused in relation to my magical practice and the practices of others. While many harms like chattel slavery, erasure of and violence against Indigenous people, and the witch burnings seem to be relegated to the past, their legacy and harm continue to this day, some more than others. Understanding where your ancestors, and you, fit into systems of oppression, both past and present, will be a big part of creating your magical ethical practice. Perhaps it already is. If not, excavating this information will be a personal journey. For example, in my practice, my distant ancestors did face religious persecution and violence, however, my more recent ancestors oppressed others in ways still playing out today. For these reasons, it's important for me to be right-sized about the harms caused in my ancestry *and* the unearned privileges I hold today that can—intentionally or unintentionally—perpetuate harm against others.

Regardless of how much you know or do not know about who your ancestors are and how they practiced magic, you can form a relationship with them today. Cultivating a meaningful ancestral relationship is not contingent upon knowing exactly who your ancestors are. There are real and meaningful ways to connect with your ancestry today, even with limited tangible information about who they were and what they did. Within this chapter, I will share practices with you to help you navigate some of the obstacles involved in forming a relationship with your ancestors. As I said, your ancestors are a part of this earth and your body. Though they may have died long ago, their energy is present and can be connected with at any time.

Your ethical practice encompasses you too. Therefore, within this chapter, we will explore magical boundaries and protection as well. You deserve the same love and care that you extend to others. Even though it might seem obvious to do this, I've found that extending my ethical practice to myself can be difficult. Fortunately, there's no shortage of ways to work with your magical practice to bolster your boundaries and sense of safety. In this same thread, I will also share some ways to work with your magical practice to engage in activism, which will certainly require a good understanding of your ancestry, ethics, boundaries, and protection magic.

I'm sure you might already see how interconnected ethics and ancestry are and, hopefully, how necessary they are to craft a well-rounded magical practice. I also want to speak to the nuance of this chapter as a European American living on stolen land. I know I will not write this chapter perfectly because internal biases affect how I experience and show up in the world. Like you, my ethical framework continues to expand, change, and grow. I am not perfect, and no matter how many times I try to get this chapter "perfect," I know it is an unattainable goal. If something I say in this chapter harms you, I want to hear about it and will take responsibility for the impact by learning and doing better if needed. Throughout this chapter, I will also share words from several Black, Brown, and Indigenous leaders and authors to offer a variety in viewpoints. I invite you to walk through this chapter tenderly, as it may stir discomfort and grief.

## Ancestral Connection

Our unique ancestries shape the connections and disconnections we experience with each other, the land, and our magical practices. The truth remains that, within each of our ancestries, there were likely wise ones who aimed to honor life as well as ancestors who caused harm to the earth and its inhabitants. Remember this as we navigate this chapter, as we can see this alive and well in real time today. We are all at different places in our journeys, and so are our ancestors. As you engage with your ancestors, part of your work will be to discern who you decide to engage with and how you engage with them, whether it be through information you read or an experience you have through a spiritual or energetic connection. This might take time, and that is okay.

You might never be able to pick up a book to read about how your ancestors practiced magic or attend a live event hosted by elders within our ancestry. Many of our ancestors passed down information orally and, at certain times throughout history, had to stop for fear of violence or due to being forcibly removed from their land and communities. It took me a long time to come to a place of acceptance, not knowing exactly how my ancestors practiced. Very few people have a direct line of information connected to their ancestors' magical and spiritual practices. If you do, treasure it! Not having this connection can be extremely painful when you want to feel connected to your ancestors. There were, and are, intentional harms that sever us from our ancestors' traditional magical practices. Understanding what these severances were and how to work with them can also help inform your connection to your ancestry. Like intuitive severances, which we'll explore in-depth in the next chapter, understanding how they impact your connection to your ancestry may be challenging. Most of us hold some level of trauma, violence, or erasure in our pasts, and looking at your ancestry forces you to engage with that pain. I want to offer the reminder that turning to the past will be one part of creating your magical practice, but not the only part.

Your ancestors' energy and presence live on in many ways. Like you, our ancestors worked with all timelines. Some prayed for their ancestors, their loved ones, and the future well-being of the planet and its inhabitants. The past, present, and future were parts of some of our ancestors' spiritual and magical practices. Your ancestors prayed for you as you may pray for your future kin and the planet's well-being. They impressed their love and magical intentions upon all timelines, and still do. Beyond timelines, your ancestors most likely worked with the land and various spirits of place. Most earth-based practitioners are animist and believe all things are living and have a soul or spirit. Due to this, it is likely that somewhere in your lineage, your ancestors impressed their magical intentions and love into the land itself. Their magical intentions remain. This also helps to explain why some have profound experiences when returning to the land of their ancestors, as if something inside a person remembers the energy of the place itself. Beyond the intent and energy of your ancestors, their physical bodies continue to be a part of the land as cycles of decomposition and regeneration continue. Your ancestors live on in the plants, trees, waters, and soil that continue to grow and flow throughout the land.

However, you might not live on the same land as your ancestors and may not even know the lands they inhabited. This is an important disconnection to name and one that many face. These severances require much nuance, especially for those of European descent, such as myself, who may be more recently active in perpetuating systems of oppression. In the recent history of the so-called United States and Canada, thousands of Native people were forced to relocate, and the repercussions of this violence continue. I live in my home state of Indiana on Native Myaamiaki land. Though some local Myaamiaki people are here, most of them were forcibly relocated to Oklahoma, far from their Native land.[2] Even though my ancestors faced colonization, many also perpetuated it. Holding these truths, I understand that I must proceed in ways that tend to my own wounding around colonization while also making active repairs for the ongoing harms caused by past and present colonization against the Native people whose land I'm on. Sadly, these harms are not unique to the United States. They have taken place all over the world and continue to do so. Part of my magical practice includes being aware of these harms to be a better ancestor and heal my own ancestral lineage. Of course, this will vary tremendously from person to person.

Beyond the physical land, there are still ways to form a living relationship with your ancestors. Within your body, the DNA of your ancestors is also a part of you. Within your blood and bones, you carry physical connections associated with those who have come before you and the land from which they came. My grandmother was born and raised in the United Kingdom and became pregnant with my father while living there. She migrated to the United States while pregnant with him. I often think about her connection to the land, her food, and the waters she drank. I know that the land became part of my father and therefore lives within me. I know that even though my body has been nourished by the land and waters of the Native people who tended the land I live on now, my body continues to hold remembrances of my ancestors. You have these same remembrances within you, even if they are more removed than mine. I also carry Irish, Scottish, Scandinavian, and German lineages and sense pings of remembrance when visiting or learning about these places.

There are many ways to connect with the living wisdom of your ancestors. Honor any written words available or traditions and teachings passed down, but don't forget to nurture the sacred responsibility to explore the wisdom of our ancestors here today by allowing new rituals and magic to evolve through you. There can be both learning and practicing old while weaving new. I'd argue there needs to be! Here you'll find a list with ideas and invitations to root deeper into your relationship with your ancestors.

For some of these suggestions, you will need to know specifics about your ancestors or the land your ancestors came from. I've also provided options for those who do not know their ancestry.

 **Ways to Engage with Your Ancestors**

- Explore the lives of the ancestors you have access to, if any.

- Learn about the foods, customs, holidays, magical practices, and lands of the places your ancestors came from.

- Make and consume foods your ancestors did.

- Connect with plants your ancestors may have worked with or that the people of those lands work with today. Do not ingest plants without discussing them with a medical professional. Do not work with plants that are part of a closed practice. Meditating or journeying to connect with a plant is an option to avoid medical and cultural appropriation concerns.

- Adopt open practices that pique your interest from your ancestors and those living on the land. Participate in closed practices only after receiving permission or appropriate rites of passage. Open practices are those that practitioners or teachers from your ancestry have stated are available for all. Closed practices are reserved for those who have received explicit permission to practice said practices. Examples of closed practices include the use of white sage and palo santo.

- Read books, learn, and seek teachings from those currently living on the land of your ancestors.

- Travel to the homelands of your ancestors.

- Create an ancestor altar, whether you know who they are or not. If this is new to you, I've included suggestions for creating one later in this chapter.

- Give offerings to your ancestors, whether you know who they are or not. In many practices, wine is a common offering, but it can also come from sacred waters, food, flowers, and more.

- Learn about the holidays, past and present, your ancestors celebrated. Practice them if they feel resonant.

- Learn about possible harms caused by your ancestors. Listen to the people who were harmed by them and what they desire for repairs. Incorporate repairing these harms as an ongoing practice.

- Learn about possible harm caused to your ancestors. Seek support and ways to heal the wounds within your lineage and yourself.

- Consider using DNA testing to learn more about your ancestry while also taking the results with a grain of salt. However, know that white supremacy is inherent in these tests; it has been shown that white people will get more nuanced results than non-white people.[3]

- Meditate or journey to connect with your ancestral lands.

- Meditate or journey to connect with your ancestors. Find a guided meditation in this chapter to do this. For a more in-depth journey, visit cassieuhl.com /meditations-courses to find an audio guided journey and workbook to connect with your ancestors.

As you connect with your ancestors, remember that, similar to the humans you engage with in the mundane world, your ancestors' personalities, demeanors, and overall wellness can vary greatly. Though it may seem radical, not everyone in spirit form is well, healed, or has your best intent. I do not say this to scare you. Rather, I wish to encourage you to approach your ancestors in the same way you might approach a stranger, which might include care, caution, and discernment. Like your living family, chosen or biological, there are probably some with whom you feel a deeper kinship. These are my personal beliefs, which you may not resonate with today or ever, but they are the lens from which I share. As always, I encourage you to form your own beliefs, but I also want you to be prepared if you encounter a spiritual connection with an ancestor that doesn't feel safe.

We each have well and unwell ancestors, and it's important to keep this in mind, especially if forming relationships with them is new to you. However, there might be times in your practice when engaging with ancestors who are unsettled or unwell can be beneficial and healing. For example, as a descendant of European settlers,

I engage carefully with some of my ancestors who've created harm and desire to learn alongside me to help heal our ancestral line. For those with different ancestries, this might not be ideal. Here is a helpful distinction from Indigenous medicine woman and author Asha Frost, who shares in her book *You Are the Medicine,* "It was more potent for me to call upon my healed and well Ancestors for my spiritual work. It protected me from taking on more responsibility or calling up heaps of trauma, which is especially important if you have a long history of suffering in your lineage." You might find that stating an intention to only connect with your well and healed ancestors before engaging is helpful. In contrast, at other times, you might find that carefully engaging with unsettled ancestors is where your energy is needed. Ultimately, I want you to know that each connection you form with an ancestor is a personal choice. I will share ways to feel better protected in your magical practice later in this chapter. Being aware of energetic protection is essential anytime you open to unseen realms.

### Ancestral Connection Meditation

I suggest blocking off 20 to 60 minutes of solitude for this meditation. Forming any relationship requires time and effort. This meditation, or a similar variation, is something to return to often.

Consider using some of these optional materials:

- Black candle and matches or a lighter
- Comforting food and drink ready for after your meditation
- Journal and pen or pencil
- Any energetic protection tools you like to use

1. Gather any materials you want to use during the meditation.

2. Spend two to three minutes connecting with your breath and body. Some ways to do this include becoming more aware of your breathing and noticing each part of your body and where you may be holding tension, shaking your limbs, or dancing.

3. Create sacred space. This could include any combination of the following: call in the elements or cast a circle, burn herbs or incense, or call in protection from your spirit guides. If you use a black candle, you can do that now too. Hold your candle, state your request to connect with your well and healed ancestors, and then light your candle. Always practice appropriate fire safety when working with candles. Never leave your candle unattended.

4. In whatever position is comfortable and accessible to you (sitting, lying down, or standing if you plan to move your body), begin to soften your gaze and close your eyes if desired. In your mind's eye and body, begin to visualize and sense a natural environment around you, such as a forest, beach, jungle, or desert. If you have a space in mind that feels intuitive and natural, go with that. If unsure, you could simply invite in a space and allow your intuition to fill in what kind of natural environment would suit you best.

5. Spend some time connecting with this space in your mind's eye. Imagine what the temperature feels like on your skin, what the earth feels like below your body, and where the sun or moon is in the sky. Become aware of any sounds within the environment, and take in the colors and textures around you.

6.  Maintain your altar and your connection to it. I liken my altars to living beings and find that treating them as such helps maintain them and my connection to them. In some practices there's reference to "feeding" an altar, which might look like pouring fresh water in a vessel, burning candles or incense, or placing food or drink on the altar. How often your altar needs to be "fed," cleansed, or maintained will vary. I encourage you to start a dialogue with your altar(s) to best determine how it would like to be maintained. Part of this maintenance will require having regular connection with your altars.

7.  Once you feel grounded and connected in the space, state aloud or within your mind's eye something like this: "I would like to connect with a well and healed ancestor."

8.  With your intent made, continue to breathe and connect with the environment around you. Remember, information may come through in a multitude of ways. You may hear words within your mind, feel sensations in your body, see a visual of a person within your mind's eye, or be transported to a different scene altogether. Be patient and try not to discount any information that comes through. Subtle connections hold value too!

9.  If you sense a connection forming and you feel safe and comfortable engaging with the ancestor that has come through, you may choose to begin communicating with them. Communication may look and feel differently than you expected. If this is your first interaction, consider viewing it as a learning experience. I encourage you to engage with curiosity.

10. Spend as much time as you'd like connecting with any ancestral energies that have come through. Listen, ask

questions, or just be with them. Remember, you will be able to come back again. Here are some questions to consider: "What are some ways that I can connect with you outside of this meditation?" "In what ways can I show my gratitude to you?" "Where can I direct my focus to learn more about you and my ancestry?"

11. When you feel ready to close this meditation, thank your ancestor for coming through. If you traveled outside of the initial natural environment, return to that natural environment first. Thank the earth for its support and grounding.

12. Open your eyes when you feel ready. Spend two to five minutes reorienting to your physical environment by looking around and possibly moving your body.

13. Consider eating and drinking some food to help connect back to the physical body and journaling about your experience.

Another way to engage with your ancestors can be through an altar. We will explore altars more in-depth in Chapter 6, but I want to share some invitations specific to engaging with your ancestors through an altar. As I mentioned, relationship-building is foundational when it comes to connecting with your ancestors. One way to build those relationships is to give offerings to your ancestors, and altars can serve as an open channel to give those offerings to them. Another purpose of an ancestor altar is to have a physical representation of them and your relationship with them. Simply put, having an ancestor altar can remind you of their presence and your relationship with them, and offer a way to engage with them regularly. The way you create your altar can be as simple or complex as you desire. It is also entirely possible that your ancestor altar and regular altar are one and the same (out of necessity or preference). Your ancestor altar might have a dedicated space year-round, and there may be situations where you want to create a temporary, possibly more elaborate, ancestor altar for a specific holiday or season like Día de los Muertos or Samhain. I am a big proponent of being creative with your altar spaces and want you to know that there's a lot of variety in how altar work is taught and practiced. Some altar practices are quite specific and strict. Here are some general guidelines for creating an ancestor altar. These are my opinions. They may or may not resonate with you or others you've learned from, and that's okay.

### Building an Ancestor Altar

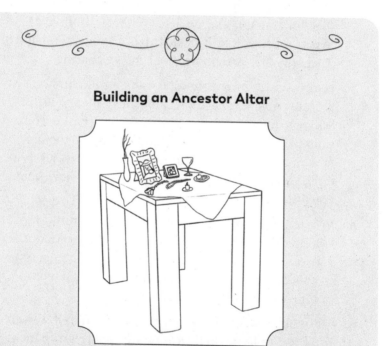

1.  Select a location for your altar. Again, this could be on a preexisting altar—this is how mine is—or a separate dedicated space. The space you select need not be large or fancy. How you engage with it is what's most important.

2.  Select any combination of items that feel resonant to you for your altar. This could include physical

items that belonged to your ancestors, photographs, artwork, representations of the four elements or single elements (water is a common element added to altars), statues or figures that you connect with your ancestry, candles, flowers, plants, herbs, magical items, and any other items that remind you of your ancestors or ancestry.

3. Energetically prepare your altar space. This might include energetically cleansing your altar space and any of the items you plan to add to it with herbal smoke, sound (bells or chimes), a broom, etc. If energy clearing is new to you, consider waiting to do this until you read Chapter 3, where you'll learn more about energy clearing.

4. Begin constructing your altar and consider inviting in any ancestors you have a relationship with and feel safe asking to join you. You might also consider asking questions like, "Where would you like this item on the altar?," "Do you want this item on the altar?," "What kinds of offerings would you like me to give you?," "How would you like to engage with me at this altar space?"

5. When the altar is complete (for now) think about whether there are any ways you feel called to honor or consecrate the altar. This could include singing a song to your ancestors, lighting a candle, giving an offering, or something else you feel inspired to do.

6. Maintain your altar and your connection to it. I liken my altars to living beings and find that treating them as such helps maintain them and my connection to them. Some practices reference "feeding" an altar, which might look like pouring fresh water in a vessel, burning candles or incense, or placing food or drink on the altar. How often your altar needs to be "fed," cleansed, or maintained will vary. I encourage you to start a dialogue with your altar to best determine

how it would like to be maintained. Part of this maintenance will require having regular connection with your altar(s).

If connecting with your ancestors is new, allow time to form relationships with them. The time it takes to form a strong connection with an ancestor could range from a few weeks to years depending on how much time you can dedicate to this practice and how connected you feel with those you meet. Remember, just like your most beloved relationships in the mundane world, some relationships will come along faster than others. Be gentle with yourself as your ancestral relationships unfold, wax, and wane. Try as many of the connection methods that feel resonant and work with the techniques often if you enjoy them. You will likely resonate with some more than others. As your relationships deepen with specific ancestors, you may sense their presence and influence in your magical workings as you connect with them more. Remember, your experiences with otherworldly realms are real. I encourage you to treat these ancestral connections as sacred.

## Cultural Appropriation

Before we discuss crafting your ethical framework for your magical practice, it's important to discuss cultural appropriation. Similar to understanding your ancestry, this topic will weave into your ethical framework. Because I am a European American and, by default, in most situations, hold more privilege, I will not be able to speak to being culturally appropriated. I will instead share words from those who have experienced cultural appropriation. What I can share is how I have caused harm through cultural appropriation, learned to do better, made repairs, and how I continue to be aware of it. As for colonization, I will primarily speak to my role as a person who is a descendant of colonizers living on stolen land.

In the beginning of my spiritual journey, I practiced yoga and eventually completed my yoga teacher training. I meditated, practiced breathwork, and considered myself Buddhist for a stint. It never dawned on me that the buffet of spiritual paths, all from cultures outside of my own and all taught to me by fellow European Americans, could be causing harm to others, let alone me. Meditation, breathwork, yoga, and Buddhism are profoundly healing and beautiful practices, which you might understandably have difficulty associating with harm. The practices are not harmful, but learning about them without understanding the impact of colonialism is. My teachers and I taught these practices in ways that were whitewashed at best and harmful at worst. For example, like many yoga teacher trainings, my training focused on physical asana with a sprinkling of the other eight limbs of yoga. Decolonial yoga teacher Susanna Barkataki speaks to this in her blog, *How to Decolonize Your Yoga Practice*, "If someone from the dominant culture completes a yoga teacher training that is primarily asana based, and remains blissfully unaware of the complexity of yoga's true aim or the roots of the practices, they are culturally appropriating yoga. By remaining unaware of the history, roots, complexity and challenges of the heritage from which yoga springs and the challenges it has faced under Western culture, they perpetuate a re-colonization of it by stripping its essence away." As a well-meaning yoga teacher, I would have never considered myself racist. Yet, the truth was the foundation of my spiritual practice was rife with white supremacy, cultural appropriation, and colonialism.

If you also adore your yoga and breathwork practices and do not have Indian ancestry, this is not a call to stop working with these practices (although a pause could be helpful). It is an invitation to dig deeper so you can experience the authentic and unimpeded depth of healing that these practices were created to offer. Doing so will help to ensure you aren't participating in the perpetuation of violent narratives. As you dig deeper, you might notice that the same means of oppression that keep you from the depth of these practices have also kept you from spiritual practices in your ancestry. It wasn't until I started investigating the effects of colonialism, white supremacy, and cultural appropriation in my practice that I realized the depth of erasure my ancestry experienced. I also had a deep cultural well of magical and spiritual practices that I could lean in to, as do you, regardless of your ancestry. These systems of oppression harm us all to varying degrees—even the people who perpetuate them. We are all worthy of unearthing and reclaiming a spiritual and magical practice in line with our ancestry, ethics, and intuition. Doing so has the potential to be radically freeing in and of itself. For some, exploring cultural appropriation in your practice might look like deep grief tending. For others, like me, it might look like divesting and making repairs. How this part of your magical practice unfolds will be unique and, hopefully, stretch beyond the pages of this book into new pathways of unlearning, relearning, healing, or repair.

Closely examining cultural appropriation in my practice looked like putting an end to my yoga teaching, eventually closing my decade-old jewelry business titled Zenned Out, halting production of jewelry rooted in cultural appropriation, publicly apologizing for any harm I'd caused, embarking on the lifelong journey of divesting from systems of oppression, and making repairs for harm caused both internally and externally.

Your path and how you make repairs, if needed, will be unique. I share this part of my journey as a transparent example of how gaining clarity around cultural appropriation can play out. Your path will likely look different. We will dive much deeper into relationship and repair in Chapter 4. Though the changes I decided to make were not always easy, they opened a pathway to create something I've desired my entire life—an unshakeable spiritual and magical practice rooted in integrity and truth.

In Rachel Ricketts's book *Do Better*, she describes cultural appropriation as "a particular power dynamic in which members of a dominant culture steal intellectual, spiritual, cultural, and/or informational wealth from a culture of people who have been systematically oppressed by that dominant group (most notably by white or white-passing folx)." She writes, "Many of the things white people practice as 'wellness' now were specifically prohibited by white people in the past. It was one of the white colonizers' many weapons of cultural destruction. Yoga being banned by Brits when they invaded India is one example[4]. Colonizers restricting the burning of sage by Indigenous tribes in North America is another. As a Black woman, appropriation causes me harm because it is yet another form of colonialism."

In Layla Saad's book *Me and White Supremacy,* she speaks to some of the nuances of cultural appropriation: "Cultural appropriation can include the appropriation of another culture's objects, motifs, symbols, rituals artifacts and other cultural elements. However, one person from one racial group can think something is culturally appropriative while another person from that same group disagrees and considers it cultural appreciation or cultural exchange." Layla Saad goes on to write more about understanding the power dynamics of cultural appropriation. She says, "The first and most important thing we need to understand, therefore, about cultural appropriation is that it occurs between a *dominant* and a *nondominant* or *marginalized* culture. To clarify, what makes one culture dominant and another nondominant has nothing to do with the specifics of the countries where those cultures are from (e.g., population size, national GDP, or how far back that culture's history goes) but rather is about the historic and present-day relationship that exists between the two cultures. We must ask ourselves whether that relationship includes colonization, land theft, mass kidnapping and enslavement, attempted genocide, forced assimilation, segregation, legalized racial discrimination, and the reinforcement of negative racist stereotypes. If so, then the culture that has benefited from this oppression is identified as the dominant one, and the culture that has suffered from this oppression is identified as the nondominant one."

Understanding cultural appropriation from a broader perspective can help you identify layers of subtlety within your magical practice. For example, suppose you identify much of your ancestry as Irish but live in the United States. In that case, it is possible to culturally appropriate native Irish spiritual practices. As Layla Saad mentioned in the previous paragraph, not everyone feels the same way about cultural appropriation, so there's value in being aware and culturally sensitive to how some folks may feel harmed by cultural appropriation. In her blog post "Question— Irish Ancestry and Cultural Appropriation?," Lora O'Brien says, "Unfortunately, part of the colonial heritage—as well as much of modern Western society—is an ingrained attitude of entitlement. I don't have that, I want that, so I am entitled to take that and do what I want with it." She continues, " . . . much of NeoPagan-ism is this way—a pick n mix of whatever the tradition's creators, or individual practitioners, need or want, taken from various [I]ndigenous cultures and traditions (and often horrifically man-gled and commercially repackaged to appeal to the lowest common denominator, in the process)." She goes on to share suggestions to avoid appropriating, "Learn from [N]ative sources . . . learn what you can from the heart of the culture you wish to connect to. Immerse yourself as much as possible in the culture and support them wherever you can. This is about walking and working in Right Relationship, wherever possible, and always endeavoring to give more than you take—to support and contribute."

In my desire to reconnect with my ancestry more deeply and ease my discomfort around feeling like I no longer had a spiri-tual "home," I started gobbling up any information I could get my hands on about the practices, past and present, of my people. I started utilizing teachings and titles that I did not fully understand in my practice. At one point, I titled my podcast *Awen*, a sacred word to many who practice in the region of my ancestors. After reflection, I realized that, in the same way that it was not okay for me to name my jewelry business Zenned Out, it also didn't feel right to title my podcast after a word that many, including me, hold sacred. You might also notice a sense of urgency arise in you as veils lift around the prevalence of cultural appropriation. I have come to learn from the several BIPOC teachers I share within this chapter, that this sense of urgency is also a tool of white suprem-acy culture. I now see it as a red flag inviting me to be more aware of where that sense of urgency might come from.

Another important layer to this topic, often discussed in tan-dem with cultural appropriation, is closed practices. Closed prac-tices are reserved for specific cultures or religions that often require rites of passage, training, or initiation. Examples that many consider closed practices are smudging with white sage, wearing a traditional headdress, and bestowing yourself with unearned titles such as "shaman," "high priestess," or "druid." This doesn't mean any practice outside your culture is closed; many practices are considered open. Even if practices are considered open, it doesn't always mean you can claim them as your own, especially if you intend to profit from them. Like cultural appropriation, understanding closed and open practices is a critical lens to consider within your ethical framework. What constitutes cultural appropriation, or closed or open practices within your magical work is not something that I can decide for you. You will need to invest time and energy into exploring your practices to determine what may or may not constitute cultural appropriation and whether or not you need to stop practicing it, keep it, or make repairs. Due to your unique ancestry, you may have been part of both dominant and nondominant cultures throughout time. You may find yourself needing to repair harms caused by cultural appropriation while simultaneously tending to wounds around others who are culturally appropriating from you. One way to become aware of cultural appropriation in your practice is to frequently examine your magical and spiritual practices. Here are some questions to consider as you do:

 ## Is My Practice Culturally Appropriating?

- Who taught me this practice?

- From what culture does the practice originate?

- Did the person who taught me this practice come from that culture?

- From whom did the person who taught me this practice learn the practice?

- Was the person they learned it from someone from the culture where the practice originated?

- Who benefits monetarily or otherwise by teaching or sharing the practice?

- Are the people of the culture the practice originated from being compensated in any way by the person teaching it, if they are outside that culture?

- Is the practice closed, or have teachers from the culture asked others to stop practicing it?

- Here's a question from Layla Saad's book: What is the history that exists between my culture and that culture?

Finding answers to these questions may not always be easy, but they are informative in crafting a magical practice rooted in integrity and ethics. I encourage you to revisit them often or add your own when learning from new people or adopting new practices. It has become a regular part of my practice to be intentional and aware when learning from new people or adopting new practices. Crafting a magical practice in this way helps end lineages of theft and exploitation. Being aware of, stopping, and making repairs for cultural appropriation does far more than repair our lineages; it also opens doorways to healing. It creates opportunities to return to our humanity in the ways we've been severed from it.

It took me nearly thirty years to get to a place where I could begin to see the damage of colonization in my magical practice. Colonization and cultural appropriation have touched all of us through being colonized, colonizing, or both, albeit to vastly different degrees and at different times. But it is there nonetheless, and, for most, it will need to be addressed to craft a personal magical practice. It's only natural that valid feelings of grief, anger, or shame might arise, regardless of who your ancestors are, as you traverse these tender topics. Teachers and healers are listed in this book's resources section for folks from different ancestral lineages. They can offer support in addressing, making repair, and healing from colonization and cultural appropriation.

Approaching these topics can be an uncomfortable part of crafting your own magic. It will probably not be a fast process either. One of my teachers, Thérèse Cator, shared in a training that "Supremacy and oppression does not want us to slow down, connect, or have space for our uncomfortable emotions to land because doing so is a threat to systems of violence." The discomfort, pain, and time associated with tending to these themes will vary from person to person, depending on each person's unique ancestry. I encourage you to explore cultural appropriation and colonization in your practice, knowing that it might be a lifelong part of your practice. You don't have to have it all figured out today. Part of unhooking my practice from oppressive systems has been learning how to be comfortable with not knowing all the right answers, understanding that making mistakes is a part of being human, and loving myself through those mistakes while making repairs when needed is essential. If you feel like you need support in the process of examining how you've culturally appropriated or been harmed by cultural appropriation, you can find resources in the back of the book.

## Crafting a Magical Ethical Framework

*Merriam-Webster's Collegiate Dictionary* defines *ethics* as "a set of moral principles: a theory or system of moral values." Understanding morals and values is where ethics can get tricky. I find the topic of morals, values, and ethics often left out or assumed in magical texts. Yet, presently, there seems to be a prevalence of cognitive dissonance, even in magical and spiritual circles. Meaning, actions and how folks appear in the world may not actually align with their morals and values. The best remedy for cognitive dissonance is knowing your morals and values so you can craft a framework of ethics that helps guide your magical practice. Cognitive dissonance tends to stem from confusion around intent versus impact. A common example is intended cultural appreciation that is actually cultural appropriation. Asha Frost speaks to this in *You Are the Medicine,* "New age and wellness communities co-opt Indigenous teachings and Medicine wisdom that is not theirs to take. Extraction in this way continues to cause harm to Indigenous communities. When people in a powerful and privileged position outside of a culture use these teachings for profit, it creates further oppression, marginalization, and pain."

Your magical workings create real change in seen and unseen realms, for better or worse, even if your intentions are good. This example illustrates why having a thoughtful and malleable ethical framework is critical. I am grateful to the teachers I've had who modeled ethics in their practices, so that when I was confronted by the harm I caused by culturally appropriating, I knew what to do. Having an ethical framework will not prevent you from ever causing harm but can alert you to when harm has been caused and provide structure for repair.

Your values and morals are deeply personal and will likely change over time. Your culture, where you live, family, ancestry, religion, etc., all influence your values and morals. Your values are formed on a personal and internal level, and help guide which morals you adhere to or value the most. Morals are commonly tied to what society has deemed as "right" or "wrong." Your values help determine which morals you may or may not align with. Ethics shows up in how you act according to your moral values. I love this explanation in the article "What Are Values, Morals, and Ethics? by Carter McNamara, "A person who knows the difference between right and wrong and chooses right is moral. A person whose morality is reflected in his willingness to do the right thing—even if it is hard or dangerous—is ethical. Ethics are moral values in action."

Limiting morals, values, and ethics to human beings alone can add more layers to ethical concerns in your magical practice. In my practice, I have learned not to rely solely on my human moral values and to widen my scope to include the plant, animal, and mineral realms. By removing my veil of human supremacy, I see a need to move beyond my human moral values and listen to those outside of my species as well—this is where relationship and reciprocity come into your ethical framework. The relationships you form with different plants, animals, and minerals might also widen your understanding of ethics. Your magical ethical framework will likely be a moving target, transforming as you do. I hope you'll leave this book with a flexible ethical framework for your magical practice that inspires you to examine your moral values often, restructure your magical ethical framework when needed, and make repairs when a situation calls for it.

I cannot tell you what your moral values and magical ethical framework should look like. What I will ask you to do is give yourself time to examine your moral values so you understand how to apply them to your magical ethical framework. The following exercise can help you get started on this journey.

### Morals, Values, and Magical Ethics Exercise

In this exercise, I will invite you to examine your moral values, list your top five, explore common magical ethical concerns, and compare those to your moral values to begin crafting your magical ethical framework.

1. Consider or journal about these questions to examine your moral values.

    - Within yourself, your community, and the world, what do you find the most troubling?

    - Within yourself, your community, and the world, what do you desire to protect the most?

    - What is important to you?

    - What are your desires for yourself, your community, and the world?

    - If you could change one thing about yourself, your community, and the world for the betterment of the earth, what would it be?

2. Based on the questions above, list your top five moral values. Keep these handy, as I will ask you to refer to them as you construct your magical ethical framework.

3. Explore this non-exhaustive list of common ethical concerns in magic and spellwork. Feel free to add more.

- Causing harm to others through magic— physically, spiritually, or emotionally

- When and how to use magic to protect vulnerable or marginalized identities

- Accessing psychic information about others without consent

- Sharing psychic information with others without consent

- Honoring free will; this shows up often in love spells when someone may try to lure another into love or attraction

- Knowing where your magical tools (e.g., crystals, herbs, etc.) are sourced from and how that sourcing might affect or harm others

- Cultural appropriation

- Lack of intersectionality

- Being unaware of social justice in magic

- Understanding how your magic and spells might affect or harm others and if it is in the best interest of all or just you

- Being non-extractive and practicing reciprocity in your magical workings—e.g., assuming the energetic or spirit world will do your bidding without giving anything in return

- Assuming hierarchy in your relationships with the animate world

4. Based on your list of moral values, which magical ethical concerns are the most important to you?

5.  Write your top ethical concerns and compare them to your current magical practices. Is cognitive dissonance showing up in your practice? If so, how might you be able to shift your practices to align your moral values with the ethics of your magical practice?

Consider what came out of this exercise as a possible foundation for your magical ethical framework. However, most importantly, do not let this initial list of ethics go unchecked. I encourage you to continue exploring your ancestry, morals, how others practice ethics in their magical workings, and how your ethics affect your magical practice and the world at large. You will make mistakes; it is a part of being human. Each time you do, it is an opportunity to assess your ethical framework and make changes. Your magical ethical framework will also be invaluable in determining what kind of magic you craft and how you craft it. Understanding the morals and values that drive your magic creates a foundation of integrity.

## Magic and Activism

When you show up in your magical practice with a firm understanding of your ethical framework, you may find that your practice needs to extend far beyond yourself and into your community. Many magical practitioners, including me, consider social justice, political involvement, or various forms of activism to be a necessary part of their practice. If your magical practice intends to bring love and healing to the world, is it truly doing that if it only includes magical workings that benefit you alone? Of course, tending to your needs is important and can create positive change in its own right. What I will encourage you to do here is to be open to ways you can use your magic to support the moral values that create your ethical framework. There are many ways to use your magic within your ethical framework to support humans and our more-than-human kin. However, in my practice, I work from the perspective that using magic in my activism does not prevent me from participating in more mundane acts such as voting or calling my local representatives. Mundane and magical acts are important and needed in regard to this topic! It's also important to note that activism work will look different for all of us. As a European American, I recognize that there is a greater need for me to listen to the voices of the global majority of humans (Indigenous, African, Asian, LatinX, Black and Brown people) and face any discomfort that might be keeping me from being a more healed and whole instrument of change. Here are some ways my magical practices weave throughout my activism.

As my practice has grown, the lines between my activism and other magical workings have blurred because I continue to find more overlap between the two as my ethical framework evolves. In my direct action within the mundane world of politics and activism, my magical practice serves as a support to help me stay rooted and engaged in work that can sometimes feel draining, frustrating, and uncomfortable. I could not engage in regular political or activism work without my magical practice, at least not from a place of love. When I am involved in activism, I devote extra time to my energy clearing, grounding, and energetic protection practices. If I don't, I know that my efforts will be short-lived or will likely cause unintended harm to others or me. I am also deeply engaged from an intuitive perspective. If you consider yourself highly sensitive, as I do, you might sometimes find yourself overwhelmed by the state of the world. When I feel like this, I tap into my intuition to help guide me to where my energy and efforts would be most supportive. When I tune in to myself, my guides, and the larger currents of energy surrounding me, I often gain a different perspective on what's happening in the world and how my magical practice might be of service.

Having the space and ability to tune in to my intuition regarding world events is a privilege I don't take lightly. I've learned that utilizing a keen sense of discernment with my intuition in instances like this is necessary. In the next chapter, we'll discuss discernment as it relates to your intuition more.

Amid intensely painful and public world events, I'm often invited to simply still myself and be with the energy of what's present before jumping into action. The dominant culture can add a false sense of urgency, even to your magical workings, especially when painful world events occur. Though it is a privilege, taking a brief pause at times like this can be a form of harm reduction. As an energetically sensitive human, you might feel an initial need to take action in your magical practice when painful world events occur. If it's accessible, I encourage you to pause and practice discernment before taking action. When I sit with my pain and discomfort first, I can tend to them and then take action from a place of being deeply nourished and rooted. For you, this might look like meditating, walking in nature, or practicing breathwork to witness and process your emotions around whatever is happening in the world. Allowing yourself time to tend to your sadness, anger, and grief in this way can help you approach activism with more compassion for yourself and others. When I see that my initial pain and discomfort are usually rooted in fear, I can better understand the fears of others who may have opposing beliefs, which allows me to show up with more empathy and love.

  **Personal Magical**
**Examples That Support Activism**

- Regular energy maintenance
- Personal protection magic
- Grounding rituals or spells
- Somatic practices
- Tuning in to your intuition before acting

## Somatic Exercise to Process Grief and Anger

Here's an exercise I work with often while engaging in activism or when I'm feeling the intensity and pain of the world and don't know how best to show up. I find that starting with my body opens up wider pathways to allow my feelings to surface and process. As with most somatic work, this exercise can stir big emotions. If you are experiencing a phase of deep loss, pain, or grief and are new to somatic work, you might find it helpful to wait or practice with the support of an experienced somatic healer. As always, adapt the exercise to suit your needs.

You'll need:

- 20–60 minutes

- Paper and writing utensils

- Optional: music, an intuitive tool like tarot or oracle cards, and food or drink for grounding post-meditation

1. Gather materials needed and prepare sacred space. If you wish, you can light incense or a candle, and/or call upon any supportive guides or allies. *Tip:* It is possible to become quite engrossed in this exercise. I often lose track of time. You might find it helpful to set a timer to sink deeper into the exercise without worrying about how long it's been or stopping at a specific time.

2. In whatever position is most comfortable for you, whether sitting, standing, or otherwise, begin to shift your energy inward. You can close your eyes if you'd like or gaze gently ahead. Begin by noticing your breath—not to change it, just to notice it. Then begin to shift your attention to any sensations you notice in your body. For example, if you

feel angry, how is that anger manifesting in your body? Does it bring a color, texture, sound, or specific sensation to mind when you notice it?

3. As you notice different bodily sensations, ask them how they want to be expressed. Expressing them could come through in many ways, including tears, movement, dance, sound, etc.

4. Continue expressing yourself in any ways that you feel inspired to, knowing that your forms of expression could change as you move deeper into this practice. For example, I often start by moving my body, then feel called to make sounds, and then the tears come. Stay with this portion of the exercise for as long as you want or are able. *Tip*: Be kind to yourself. This practice is not about looking or sounding how the dominant culture might describe as "good" or "pretty." This exercise is about moving your body and emoting how it wants or needs to, regardless of how it looks. Moving and making sounds like this might initially feel uncomfortable, and that's okay; it can get easier with practice.

5. When you feel ready to begin moving out of the somatic portion of this exercise, start slowing down; and when you're ready, sit or lie down. Again, focus your attention inward, return to your breath, and notice how your body feels. Notice if any shifts have taken place.

6. When you feel ready, begin orienting yourself to your physical space. I like to slowly look around my room to help do this. If you have food and drink ready, this might be a good time to have it. I usually have food and drink nearby to help me come back to my physical surroundings.

7.  When you feel ready, consider writing about what came up for you during the somatic part of this exercise. These are some reflections to consider: *What came up initially? How did it feel in my body? How did it want to be expressed? How did it feel to express it in these ways? How does my body feel after this experience? What insights surfaced as a result?*

8.  You might have different questions or thoughts as a result of this exercise. Working with intuitive tools can sometimes be supportive at this point. You might like to do this by connecting with a guide or magical ally or using an intuitive tool such as a pendulum, tarot cards, or oracle cards. If you do work with your intuition at this point, consider recording your findings in a journal.

9.  When this exercise feels complete, close the practice in a way that feels supportive to you. This could include thanking yourself and any guides or allies that came through, closing your circle, or simply allowing a few moments of silence to acknowledge the experience.

When approaching activism from non-ordinary reality and creating shifts and changes in the unseen realms, I rely on completely different forms of magic that are more collaborative. Here are some examples:

## Collaborative Magical Examples That Support Activism

- Turning to your magical relationships and community for guidance and direction prior to taking action

- Directing supportive or healing energy to those experiencing a tragedy (human-made or natural)

- Crafting protection magic (distance or in-person) for groups of people, animals, or plants

- Tuning in to energetic collective themes of energy to assist in ushering new waves of energy in or out

- Placing physical, magical items or spells in specific locations for collective protection, support, or love

I realize that some of these might seem rather "out there" to some. These practices have come to me through my relationships with my guides and more-than-human kin. A theme that has surfaced as a result of crafting my own magic and applying it to my ethical framework is the reminder that magic is powerful. It can have far-reaching effects, and I should let it be as powerful and impactful as I'm guided to. Large-scale work like this is always done collaboratively and not with me at the helm.

If you feel moved to create a larger umbrella of magic for a group needing support, healing, or protection, I want to stress the importance of care, discernment, and respect. I find this especially important when those involved may not know that you're crafting magic on their behalf, when you're working magic for the environment and for communities of people you are not a part of. Humans are, for the most part, causing quite a bit of harm to the earth. Therefore, if you feel called to craft magic on behalf of the environment, you might find it helpful and enlightening to consult the land, plant, and animal beings before doing it. This same sentiment would also apply to a person who holds privilege crafting magic for communities experiencing oppression. For white folks, this is often referred to as "white saviorism"[5] and it also applies to our magical workings. As Regina Jackson and Saira Rao explain, "White saviorism is so embedded in our cultural psyche that you might not even realize it." For example, when it comes to offering up my magic directly toward BIPOC, I will not craft magic, even if I have the best intentions, unless I receive a direct invitation to do so. If it is unclear whether or not I should apply magical or energetic practices in a situation regarding others, I relegate my support to mundane assistance, such as bringing awareness, protesting, and political engagement. Of course, your magic can help support you in these mundane efforts! Again, knowing how your magic might affect those around you is key.

Early in my practice, while discussing ethics with one of my mentors, she offered a visualization practice of blanketing a person or area in loving energy to offer gentle love and support without being intrusive or tinkering with the specifics of a situation. This is a simple but powerful practice I use regularly. I've also similarly offered love and support while working with candles. You might think of another way that works well for you. There are ways to incorporate magic and activism that do not include forcing outcomes or acting as if your way is the only correct way. I often find myself offering gentle love and support via my magical practice to the people I disagree with the most, as it helps me locate deeper compassion. Alternatively, you will likely find situations where specific magic is helpful and needed in your activism. For example, if I am participating in a protest or direct action, I might create a sigil or a charm bag to place at the location because it is discreet and easy to bring along. In doing this, I can craft it in a way that invites anyone who feels they need protection to tap into it, whether they know I've offered it or not. If working with sigils or charm bags is new to you, that's okay; they are not the only ways to craft magic for protection. Throughout this book, you will find ways to access, identify, and hone your own methods to craft magic for various purposes. As you allow your ethical framework to guide your magical practice, you will have many opportunities to open yourself to new and creative ways to bring support and healing to the beings—human and more-than-human—who desire it.

## Boundaries and Protection Magic

In Chapter 3, we'll discuss energy maintenance as the defensive practice of shifting your energy to feel more embodied and better able to access your intuition. The offensive counterpart to energy maintenance is protection magic, which can also include boundaries. Protection magic and boundary setting are the proactive things you do in your practice to protect yourself (mentally, physically, emotionally, and energetically) from outside situations and forces. Protection magic can also extend far beyond yourself and be worked for others, human and more-than-human. I find that the more mundane act of setting boundaries and magical acts of energy protection support each other beautifully. As usual, weaving the mundane and the magical can instill greater depth into your practice.

A proactive protection practice can help you feel more grounded and supported in your magical practice and your ethical framework can help inform it. When you lack energetic protection, you might find yourself in perpetual cycles of confusion, lack of agency, and overgiving, and find yourself emotionally and physically drained. As a result, you might produce sloppy magic that doesn't serve you or anyone.

Your boundaries extend far beyond the mundane world. For various reasons, you will likely need to apply them to your relationships with your spirit guides, magical allies, and ancestors. For example, you might have ancestors still working through trauma that you're not ready or willing to face, or you may need to ask for a break from your spirit guides to protect your mental and emotional well-being. Sometimes, enforcing boundaries in your energetic and magical relationships is acceptable and necessary. Furthermore, not having a solid awareness of your boundaries may indicate how you approach the boundaries of others in ordinary and non-ordinary reality. In this section, we'll explore how to determine what kinds of protection magic might best serve you and others as well as energetic protection basics and how boundaries can support them.

How you decide to weave boundaries and protection magic into your practice will be unique to your ancestry, ethical framework, and personal needs. What works for me may not work best for you. I encourage you to examine your need for boundaries and protection from these lenses. Having a good understanding of your energy maintenance practice will also help, which we'll delve into in the next chapter. If you find yourself using all of your energy maintenance techniques every time you come home from work, it's a good indication that protection magic and better boundaries might be beneficial. You might find that protection magic and setting boundaries are a more efficient and loving way to care for yourself spiritually, emotionally, and physically. As someone who identifies as highly sensitive, I see protection magic and setting boundaries as ways to lighten the load of my energy maintenance practice. Your ethical framework can help you when determining your boundaries and protection magic. For example, If you are firmly rooted in your moral compass, you will know where and how you want to allocate your time and energy. You can utilize your boundaries and protection magic to ensure you can tend to the things you've deemed most important. Let's start by exploring boundaries in your magical practice.

Understanding my magical practice and ethics has helped me create firm and supportive boundaries that I rarely need to share with others. The most effective boundaries are seldom spoken or shared but acted upon. Boundaries like this might include not purchasing items from companies you know to be harmful, committing to allocate a certain amount of money each month to mutual aid, or limiting your time on social media. Boundaries are often talked about in relation to other people, but applying them to how you spend your time can be deeply supportive in your life and magical practice. Recognizing that privilege plays a role in setting boundaries is equally important. Not everyone has equal access to set boundaries, especially concerning comfort. Race, culture, disability, sexual identity, and more affect people's access to safety and ability to set boundaries. Alternatively, setting boundaries will not always be about ensuring comfort for some. If you hold unearned privilege, always setting boundaries for comfort could turn into a bubble of toxic positivity. Creating your boundaries through the lens of your consciously crafted ethical framework can help you root your boundaries into your core values. Crafting boundaries from your core values could mean that not all of your boundaries feel good; they might even leave you feeling discomfort. For example, some people may respond negatively if you've set a boundary to wear clothes that make you feel good but do not align with the dominant culture. Boundaries can't always protect you from feeling bad, but they can help you align yourself with your core values. Here are some questions to reflect on or use as journal prompts to explore your boundaries;

 **Journal Prompts to Examine Your Boundaries**

- What people, places, and activities (mundane and magical) affect your energy the most?

- Based on your list from the above question, where do you have the ability to set boundaries?

- What boundaries would be the most doable and supportive for your energetic well-being?

- How might your magical practice help?

- Do these boundaries align with your ethical framework?

- In reflecting on your magical ethical framework, what boundaries could you set to better support it?

- How could you utilize your magical practice to support the boundaries listed in the previous question?

- If some of your boundaries agitate your nervous system, how might you lean on your magical practice to support you?

- Where and how might your boundaries need to come into play in your magical practice?

Protection magic can be a helpful support when you're in situations where you're unable to set boundaries or they simply are not honored. There are, unfortunately, many situations where this happens personally, collectively, and in the more-than-human world. Protection magic can help. This is another topic in which entire books have been written. If you feel like you need greater protective magic, I encourage you to focus your energy on your closest magical guides and allies to begin collaborating in this way, which we'll explore more in this book. Protection magic often involves warding off, blocking, and banishing specific energies, actions, or people through spellwork or rituals. Protection magic can be as simple as wearing a protective talisman or as elaborate as creating unique spell bags to be placed in specific locations. When my family moved across the country, I created protective charm bags for me and my family and put great care into each one. I don't do this every time we drive somewhere, but it felt important to have extra protection for such a big journey. Not only was our cross-country move seamless—and I credit some of that ease to my protective charm bags—but it also gave me a sense of ease knowing they were in place. The complexity of your energetic protection practice will vary situationally. Like energetic maintenance, I encourage you to try different techniques individually to determine which methods work best for you. Here are some common ways that protection magic can be utilized:

## Protection Magic Practices

1. **Symbols and sigils:** Symbols and sigils (symbols imbued with unique magical energy) are common in protection magic because they're so easy to place in specific areas. I love working with these forms of magic when protecting a physical location. They are also ideal for threshold spaces, like doorways and windows, where you might need greater protection. There are many culture-specific symbols used in protection magic. On the other hand, sigils are images you create in collaboration with your magical allies to imbue them with specific energy. Symbols and sigils can be discrete and still offer protection. For example, I often draw symbols and sigils on doorways with saltwater anytime I move.

2. **Calling upon guides, allies, and ancestors:** Calling upon various helper spirits to offer protection is great because it is so accessible that you do not need any physical items to request protection. You will require an established relationship with the spirits you're calling upon. Relationships like this could be with Gods or Goddesses, well ancestors, spirit guides, or other magical allies you've formed connections with. As your community of magical relationships grows, you'll likely find that whom you call upon or who shows up for protection will vary situationally. For example, when I embark on a spiritual journey, I ask which guides or allies want to come along for protection and guidance. Sometimes, just one will come, while other times, for more treacherous journeys, everyone might come along. I use a similar system when I feel unsafe in a physical setting. Doing so will usually require a few mindful breaths to tune in to

my body before asking for help, but I know that my magical allies and guides are always present to assist when needed. Being able to call upon your magical allies is a gift of creating a practice rooted in reciprocal relationships. If the relationship is already there, asking for help comes more easily.

3. **Protective stones and minerals:** Stones and minerals are common collaborations when asking for protection. Several minerals and crystals, like black tourmaline, hematite, obsidian, amethyst, and salt are commonly worked with for physical and energetic protection. Working with stones and minerals can protect your energy field or larger areas, especially when working with multiple stones to create a grid or a perimeter. My invitation to call upon these minerals for assistance in protection would be to form a relationship with them and ask them if and how they might like to help. I try not to make assumptions when it comes to protection. You will likely find that these minerals are happy to assist but might also require some form of reciprocity, including regular charging or clearing. Though countless books offer guidance around working with crystals and minerals, remember your personal relationship with them is also valid. You might find that a stone you encounter on a walk offers more protection than an expensive polished stone from the other side of the world.

4. **The elements:** Working collaboratively with all the elements for protection is a common practice among witches, pagans, and many Indigenous cultures. It may or may not align with your ancestral roots. If you find that working with the elements is supportive in your practice, I invite you to explore working with them in your protection magic. In many practices, calling upon the four or five elements might be called "casting a

circle" or "calling the quarters." It is a way to create an energetic protective bubble while you practice magic or embark on journeys in non-ordinary reality. Once you have established a relationship with the elements, you might also feel comfortable calling upon them for protection in larger spaces.

Working with protection magic and boundaries offers a means of feeling more safe, secure, and supported in your magical prac-

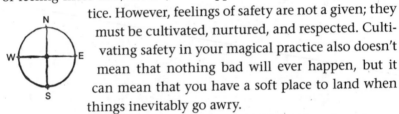

tice. However, feelings of safety are not a given; they must be cultivated, nurtured, and respected. Cultivating safety in your magical practice also doesn't mean that nothing bad will ever happen, but it can mean that you have a soft place to land when things inevitably go awry.

Though the element of earth appears solid, still, and unchanging, it is not. Yes, you can find a sense of stability in the steadiness of the earth, but it is also our regenerative teacher showing us how to integrate what is no longer needed and how to be reborn. The earth shows us how to sit in silence with death, destruction, and the muck we so often avoid. Like the unrelenting darkness and cold of winter, there's an invitation to be fully present with what we can't control and perhaps even despise. The earth knows that there's nourishment in the unknown of death. Once transformed, death becomes the compost from which a new cycle will begin, again and again and again. May your relationship with your ancestors and ethical framework be as generative as the compost that births new life. With a strong foundation, we'll begin exploring the importance of intuition in your magical practice.

CHAPTER 3

# AIR:
## INTUITION

*"Practice listening to your intuition, your inner voice; ask questions; be curious; see what you see; hear what you hear; and then act upon what you know to be true. These intuitive powers were given to your soul at birth."*

— Clarissa Pinkola Estés, Ph.D.,
*Women Who Run with the Wolves*

Intuition and magic are sometimes considered to be completely separate topics. For example, some books on magic will remove intuition entirely and instead offer scripted recipes and anecdotes. In comparison, intuition is reserved for the psychic, seer, and oracle. As you'll see throughout this book, when crafting your own magic, you will likely find it necessary to have a deep relationship with intuition. Crafting your own magic will ask you to rely on the intuitive currents nearest and within you to form a magical practice that aligns with your local environment, your ancestral lineage, and the relationships you form within the physical and spiritual planes. However, you may find times when it is helpful or necessary to lean on others as a guide in your magical practice. I've found that relying more on my intuitive insights from my magical relationships with various more-than-human beings and less on other humans deepens my magical practice's wisdom, trust, and potency. Working this way is not the fast route, but it places the power of your magical practice back into your hands.

Intuition is something we all have access to and are born with. The concept of intuition, as we'll explore it here, encompasses two parts: intuitive energy, the ever-present

currents of otherworldly information all around us; and our intuitive abilities, the way we step into those streams of energy and
feel it manifest in our bodies. Usually, it's not long before our
awareness of intuitive energy and ability to recognize it is mas-
saged from our minds and bodies. *Remembrance* and *agency* are
two words I invite you to hold as we explore intuition. Another
invitation I want to offer you is that your body, and your relationship with it, is a powerful portal to accessing intuition. Your
body, and all of its seasons, is not something to be transcended; it
is the key. The theme of reclaiming cycles will weave throughout
this book, including the topic of intuition. Your intuitive abilities
translate through the body; therefore, having an intimate awareness of your body will be important. Like the moon, your physical
vessel moves through various cycles and seasons. Understanding
the language of your seasons and how it relates to your intuitive
abilities can create a roadmap that allows you to be more in sync
with the intuitive energy around you and within you. Sometimes,
your body will require more rest or solitude, whereas other times,
you may feel a pull to movement and communal activities.

There are endless ways to access intuitive energy because it is
pervasive. This means that sometimes you might be better able
to access intuitive energy by quietly lying on the earth, while
other times, you might receive guidance from a child's mouth.
The inability to honor our bodies' cycles is often intentional and
prevents us from being consistently plugged into the ever-present
currents of intuitive energy. You are likely not doing anything
wrong if you feel out of touch with your intuitive abilities. We
were never intended to work 40- to 60-hour workweeks, stare at
screens for hours a day, or have food insecurity. For the most part,
the barriers you may face around honoring the seasons of your
body are by design and do not affect all people equally. In this
chapter, I will encourage you to find ways within your body, the
earth, and the deep wisdom of your ancestors to remember how to
connect with the ever-present stream of otherworldly information
we all have access to, even in realities that try to sever us from it.

Like the element of air, intuitive energy is an invisible and intangible force that resists containment in our physical world. Intuition

is nonlinear and does not abide by binary thinking. It lives inside you and outside of you. It can be stepped into or invoked. It is non-physical but is simultaneously expressed through the physical world and our bodies. Like a feather gently rolling in the wind, intuition relishes in being courted but rarely abides by mundane rules. To further the mystery of intuition, how you experience it will be quite personal. Like the variety of air, which can present as gentle, intense, still, warm, or cool, etc., the way you experience intuition will be varied and unique. It will also change over time. I believe that much of our fascination with intuition resides in its intangible and unnamable qualities. Intuition is like the spiritual realm's dark matter, an ever-present energy current that continues to pull us in to explore and know it more intimately, but simultaneously resists our human boundaries. How do we begin courting such an elusive and uniquely personal quality? One way is to honor and accept the inherent mystery of intuition.

I cannot tell you what your intuition will feel like or how it will present because it will be unique to you. Instead, I can guide you to discover how your intuitive abilities want to be approached and worked with in your unique body that carries a story of its own. I will share stories of my personal experience with my intuition to illustrate the diversity of intuitive abilities, not to claim to know what is best for you. Intuition and psychic abilities are available to all of us. Though some may come into this physical existence with a natural ability, just like learning a new instrument, everyone can practice and learn how to engage with their intuitive abilities. Whether yours came more naturally, you are new to exploring, or you're somewhere in the middle, having a deep understanding of intuition will be a significant part of crafting your own magic. If you are well seasoned in your intuitive abilities, I invite you to come along and explore the possibilities of new ways to engage intuition throughout this chapter. As someone who came into this world with open psychic and intuitive abilities, I am no longer surprised when my intuition evolves. I understand my intuition, like air, to be intangible and on the move.

When learning how to mend something like intuitive ability that's been so disregarded in so many of us from a young age, learning how to trust it can feel challenging and deeply vulnerable. This is not only normal, it is to be expected. You will not always be right about your intuition. And anyone who claims to be, in my opinion, is probably not trustworthy! Humans are fallible, and so are our intuitive abilities. Learning to navigate perfectionism in any subject can feel icky; intuition is no different. You won't always get it right because intuitive energy is translated through the physical body. According to a 2016 study, 70 percent of adults have experienced a traumatic event in their lifetime.[1] We also know that trauma affects the body.[2] This is just one layer of accessing and interpreting intuition. I offer this as a reminder to be gentle as you navigate this process. As someone who's felt naturally intuitive for my entire life, I still have moments (sometimes weeks and months!) of vulnerability and discomfort around the decisions I make because of intuitive insights. You will likely find grief and themes of shadow work while learning to deepen and trust your intuitive abilities. Beyond understanding the nuance of intuition in our modern world, you will also learn practices for building an intuitive foundation and creating an intuitive language between you and the spirit realm. You'll find out how to develop discernment while working with your intuition, establish energetic maintenance, and find ways to lean in to your intuition more regularly.

## Building an Intuitive Foundation

In this section, I will focus on two facets of building an intuitive foundation. I've found that breaking down intuition into understanding these two facets is helpful in a field that I believe has been made far more confusing than it needs to be. The first is understanding what helps you move into the stream of intuition. The second is understanding how that current of intuition manifests itself in your body. If this sounds different from what you've been told about intuition, stick with me.

Many spiritual and magical practices cross-culturally describe intuition as something one can step into. This is why I differentiate between intuitive energy and intuitive abilities. Intuitive energy is what you can move into, and your intuitive abilities are how you discern what that energy is expressing. There's an undeniable underlying theme in many spiritual practices of an ever-present stream of information available to us. To have a baseline understanding of intuition as something you can be outside of or in flow with, you have to put yourself in the flow of it regularly to determine what it looks and feels like for you. In Druidic practices, this stream of information is called Awen. Author and Druid Penny Billington describes Awen in her book *The Path of Druidry* as a "source of inspiration from the other realms." In Hinduism and some Buddhist practices, this stream of information is referred to as Akāśa or Akasha. In many Indigenous practices, this intuitive energy resides in plants, trees, animals, and the land itself. Many magical traditions worldwide have words to describe the flow of spiritual or intuitive energy streams that one can call upon or move into. You may find it beneficial to seek out books or practitioners unique to your lineage to learn about possible words used to describe these intuitive streams of information. Or you can experiment and notice what streams of intuitive energy are available to you where you live. I've found it's more important to experience these currents of intuitive information than to call them by a "correct" name. Streams of inspirational and intuitive energy exist with or without our human desire to name and claim them.

Shifting your understanding of intuition as something constantly flowing in and around you, rather than something you either have or don't have, is critical when building a foundation. As you engage intuition, it becomes less about being "good" or "bad" at it and much more about putting yourself in the flow of it often so you can better recognize it. These streams of inspiration are here, whether or not you choose to engage with them. In fact, you've likely experienced the sensation of being in the flow of intuition, regardless of intentionally trying to. These energy currents can be tapped into or stepped into through dance, art-making, being in nature, or slowing down and noticing your breath. Can you recall the last time you witnessed a sunset that took your breath away or smelled a flower that instilled a sense of awe? How did you feel? Did time seem to slow down? Did you feel more connected to the world around you? Did you have a sense of deep peace? Or, maybe you've experienced a sudden jolt of intuitive information walking into a new space where you innately knew it was where you were supposed to be or needed to leave. Experiencing the flow of intuition in this way may cause you to stop and pause physically. These are all common sensations when one moves into or invokes intuitive energy. A common thread between them is an undeniable shift in how you perceive and experience the world around you.

The second part of understanding intuition involves knowing how it manifests or feels in your body, which will vary for everyone. Intuition rarely speaks in words, although it can. It speaks in feeling, internal knowings, visions, color, sound, sensations, words, and taste. It can be fast, slow, quiet, or loud. How it shows up for you will likely change over time. Identifying how intuition moves through your vessel will be a large part of building your intuitive foundation. The best way to understand how it shows up in your unique body is by putting yourself into the intuitive flow often. Intuitive information is often, but not always, quieter than the noise of the mundane world. It requires a subtle shift in perception from the outer world to your inner landscape. This shift in perception does not always mean slowing down, though it can. I liken it to a dial where I turn my focus on the outer world down and my awareness of my inner sensations up. We live in a world of attention economics where companies pay to keep you from your inner landscape. There are many forces aimed at keeping you from being in this more perceptive state and being able to shift into it, at will, is something to nurture with deep care and respect. This is why taking the time to understand what helps you move into a more receptive state is so important when it comes to building an intuitive foundation. Let's explore some ways to put yourself into the flow of intuition. Then we can circle back to ways to discern how it shows up in your body.

This is a short list of ways to help you move into a more receptive state to sense the currents of intuition within and around you. Perhaps you already know how to shift into a receptive state, or maybe some of the techniques on this list are new to you. I invite you to try what speaks to you the most and consider getting a little out of your comfort zone. Many of these techniques have entire books written about them, so you can dig deeper if you want. I've also included a step-by-step activity for working with nature as a muse to move into the flow of intuitive energy.

 **Ways to Put Yourself in the Flow of Intuition**

- Get outside or go for a mindful walk

- Chant or sing

- Take time for conscious rest

- Meditate

- Listen to music

- Make music

- Create art

- Do somatic exercises such as dance or gentle movement

- Engage in breathwork

- Work with plant medicine*

- Use intuitive tools such as tarot or oracle cards, a pendulum, scrying, etc.

*Always seek the support of a trained herbalist or medical professional before ingesting plants that you aren't familiar with.*

## Outdoor Mindfulness Practice to Step into the Intuitive Flow

Cross-culturally, connecting with nature is a common way to connect with intuitive energy. This activity can be done in any environment—urban, suburban, or rural. A tree in a parking lot can have as much wisdom to share as one in a forest. You do not need to walk, and you can certainly opt to practice this sitting outside. Modify this exercise as needed to suit your unique needs and body.

1. Decide on an outdoor location to sit or walk through. If you feel particularly called to a specific location and it is accessible, go there.

2. As you walk or sit, spend one to three minutes noticing your breath and body. You could ask yourself questions to tune in to your body like, *Where is my breath, and how does it feel in my body today?"* or *"Are there any sensations inside my body that would like to let themselves be known?*

3. When you feel tuned in to your body, notice how your environment might affect your physical and energetic

body. Notice the temperature of the air, sounds around you, what the earth feels like beneath your feet, and any colors or textures around you.

4. Continue this awareness practice as you walk, or move your gaze as you sit. Notice whether your attention is pulled toward certain areas or objects. If you feel your attention pulled somewhere in your immediate surroundings, honor it by moving toward it or by directing your gaze there.

5. As you move into different areas or your eyes rest on different areas, become aware of any subtle shifts or changes in your body. For example, if you feel called to move closer to a body of water, do you feel any changes within yourself, such as seeing different visuals (in the mind's eye or within the physical world), sensations in the body, words flowing through your mind, or sensations on your skin?

   *Tip:* Try not to discount any information that comes in as you commune with your environment. Many of us have been conditioned to discount intuitive information as just "something made up." Intuition can be subtle and may require that you suspend judgment.

6. If you feel you've made an intuitive connection with the environment or something within it, I invite you to go a step beyond intuition, into connecting with spirit. Consider asking a question. You could ask anything. Here are some suggestions: "Tell me about yourself." "Do you have anything to share with me?"

7. Again, tune back in to your body and scan for shifts or changes.

8. Continue this back-and-forth dialogue or move to a new area to repeat the process as long as you desire.

9. When you feel ready to disengage from an intuitive connection, if it feels safe to do so, I invite you to thank whomever you were exchanging information with.

10. When you're ready to return to your day, you may feel it is appropriate to do another body scan. Doing so can be a helpful gauge of how this experience may have shifted your physical body. It can also be a good energy hygiene practice to ensure you're not leaving with any unwanted energetic imprints. See the section for energetic protection and clearing for more information.

11. Consider writing about your experience in a journal.

## Consistency Is Key

Consistent practice will make understanding how your body interprets and translates intuitive information easier. However, I want to gently offer that consistency doesn't mean perfection. The energy you have to build your intuitive foundation will wax and wane. That's okay. It doesn't matter how old you are, how nonintuitive you think you are, or how consistent you've been in the past with an intuitive practice. You can begin or revisit building an intuitive practice at any stage of life, and you deserve to!

You may find it helpful to determine what consistency looks like for you. I invite you to think about what feels like a nourishing *and* doable amount of time engaging in intuitive activities. Perhaps for you, it's 10 minutes a day, an hour twice a week, or 30 minutes every other day. It will look different for everyone, including you, throughout different phases of your life. I have gone through several phases where my intuitive practice has paused for months or even years. Phases of deep grief or transformations may force you to pause your intuitive and magical practice, and that's normal. The important thing is that you come back. The magical current of intuition and your spiritual guides will always welcome you back with open arms.

You will likely find that a combination of the methods shared above will serve you well as you construct or broaden your intuitive foundation. If making art is one way that you know helps move you into the flow of intuition, but it isn't doable for you to make art every day, perhaps you can do that sometimes and can focus on breathwork and meditation for 10 to 15 minutes on other days. You may find working with various techniques to get you into a flow consistently is helpful. Try what speaks to you the most.

If you're new to learning how your intuition presents, you may notice subtle changes in your mind, emotions, and body as you consistently practice activities that make you more receptive to intuitive energy. This is a sign that your intuitive abilities are waking up or increasing in intensity, although they may be very subtle in the beginning. For example, if you're focusing on your breathing, you may notice a subtle sense of feeling more connected to your body and the space around you. You may begin to notice a warming or tingling sensation in your heart space. The tone of your inner dialogue might change, or you might begin to see visions within your mind's eye. You might find it helpful to have a journal to record what comes up as you practice moving into receptive states more regularly. Doing so can make it easier to identify patterns in your unique intuitive abilities.

## The Clair Senses

The clair senses are a common way of describing how intuitive information can present in your body. Though I do use this system as a way to understand and explain sensing intuitive information, the clairs are not the only ways psychic information presents itself and can therefore be limiting. However, it is a great starting place and an easy way to understand how intuitive energy can present itself.

**Clairvoyance or clear seeing:** Seeing intuitive information within the mind's eye or in real life as colors, patterns, or visuals

**Clairsentience or clear feeling:** Feeling intuitive information within the body as emotions or feelings

 **Claircognizance or clear knowing:** Experiencing an inner knowing of intuitive information

**Clairaudience or clear hearing:** Hearing intuitive information through words, sounds, or music as inner dialogue or external sounds

 **Clairtangent or clear touching:** Receiving intuitive information by way of one of the other clairs when you place your hands on or touch something, also called psychometry

**Clairgustance or clear tasting:** Receiving intuitive information through taste

 **Clairalience or clear smelling:** Receiving intuitive information through scent

As you continue to lean in to your unique intuitive abilities, you will likely notice that they shift and change over time. I've found this to be a normal part of my practice and now relish learning new ways that intuitive information can move through my body, mind, and spirit. As someone who usually experiences intuition through visuals in my mind's eye, I've been encouraged by my spiritual allies to lean more deeply into sensations and feelings in my body. I've found that my mind can be quite limiting when translating information from the spiritual realm. Sometimes, the formless and wordless sensations felt in my body can transmit information more concisely. I encourage you to be open to how you interpret and engage with intuitive energy as your abilities cycle through different phases over time.

## Repairing Intuitive Severances

Intuitive severances are moments within your ancestry and current lived experience when you or your ancestors were severed from your magical, intuitive, and spiritual practices due to oppression, colonization, religious persecution, assimilation, or violence. Intuitive severances can occur to everyone regardless of race, gender, or ancestry. They can occur by choice, out of self-preservation, or force. You may have experienced intuitive severances as a child, in your ancestral line, in the present, or a combination. Depending on where you live, where you come from, and your connection to your ancestors, you've likely experienced some intuitive severances. In my opinion, these can impact your intuitive abilities, even if they happened to ancestors hundreds or thousands of years ago.

Like much of what we've discussed, the recency and intensity at which these kinds of severances have occurred have not been equal across all people. With current power dynamics such as white supremacy, colonization, and patriarchy, many groups of people face intuitive severances, among many other harms, today or have done so in their recent past. As discussed in Chapter 2, it is crucial to be aware of how these power dynamics may present in your current lived experience to ensure that your magical practice does not cause more harm to you or others. For example, though Europeans and European Americans like me, especially women, experienced painful intuitive severances during the burning times when an estimated 50,000-plus women were executed[3], it is essential that they not overshadow the need to end present-day oppression and harm causing the same kinds of intuitive severances and violence today. It is possible to heal and acknowledge oppression in your past while acting in solidarity for the liberation of others today. *Both can exist.*

These power dynamics and systems of oppression naturally make many feel mentally unstable, fearful, or distrustful about their intuitive experiences. For example, if you witnessed a loved one being physically harmed or, worse, killed due to them sharing their intuitive insight or healing abilities, you would probably think twice about voicing or acting upon your intuitive insights. Yet, smaller severances occur to many magically and intuitively inclined folks regularly too. For example, I felt called to work with the tarot as a teenager. After purchasing my first deck, my mother quickly informed me that it was against the Bible and related to the devil to work with the tarot. Though I kept my deck, a lingering fear stayed with me around working with the tarot well into my adulthood. We can also see present-day examples of this in our language. For example, *lunatic,* which is the root word relating to the moon, and *hysterical,* the root word relating to the womb, are now words used to describe someone as being mentally unstable. The moon and the womb are places of power and intuition for many women, womb bearers, and magical practitioners. The fractures implicated by these words have no doubt had a detrimental effect on many, and they are just one small example of how even our language continues to try to sever us from our intuitions. I will not go through all the ways in which these present-day systems and past traumas may affect you personally because it will vary for everyone due to your unique past. I will share a personal story to illustrate how an ancestral intuitive severance showed up as needing to be healed in my magical practice.

During an intensely transformative time in my life and intuitive practice, I embarked on a spiritual experience that changed how I relate to my intuition. During an energy work session that I was facilitating with a client, an erratic and deeply fearful older woman appeared to me and did not want me to continue working with this client, as if she were trying to protect her, or us. It is common for ancestors and guides to show up with messages for my clients in my work, though they're generally not as intense as this woman was being, so she certainly got my attention! When I shared about this woman, my client had no idea who it could be. I shrugged it off as a simple miscommunication between me and this ancestor. The following day, I embarked on a spiritual journey (journeying is a technique akin to meditation, which we will explore more in the next chapter) to connect with my ancestors. When I arrived in the otherworld area where I connect with my ancestors, the wild and fearful woman was there. I now understood she was for me, not my client, and was a distant ancestor. She approached me again with her same intensity and fear, waiving her arms around and begging me to stop. It was in that moment that I realized she believed she needed to protect me from deepening my connection with my intuition and magic for fear that it would put me in harm's way. She had undoubtedly witnessed this in her lifetime and wanted to protect me from the same kind of harm. I stayed with her for a long time, simply witnessing her fear and pain. I thanked her for her concern and her desire to protect me and left to return at a later time.

After taking some time to process these experiences, I journeyed again to connect with her. This time I was prepared to love, thank, and release her. I recognized her fear and discomfort as a very real part of me that needed to honor the grief that so many who came before me felt as a result of not being able to express their spiritual, intuitive, and magical abilities. Eventually, wise and healed ancestors and guides of mine came forward to help honor this woman and help her find peace. Beautiful flowers appeared, and I knew it was time to put this woman and the part of her that lived on in me to rest. I created a grave for the woman and told her it was safe for her to rest and that I no longer needed her to protect me in this way. For the remainder of the journey, my ancestors, guides, and I placed flowers all over her body to thank and honor her, this part of me, and all those who came before in my lineage who did not feel safe honoring their intuitions or magical practices. The wild and fearful woman represented an intuitive severance that likely happened hundreds of years ago in my ancestral lineage. If you harbor feelings of unease, distrust, or fear of your intuition, you might carry a similar intuitive severance.

The shifts that this experience created within my spiritual and magical practice were profound. I had a newfound trust in my intuitive abilities and a sense of freedom to express them. Shortly after this experience, I had one of the most intense spiritual experiences of my life. I don't doubt that I would not have been willing or able to experience the intensity of it had I not first released some of my fear around my intuition that was buried deep within my ancestral line. Today, in my practice, I still have uncertainty at times, but it is less frequent. When it does happen, I can return to this experience and remind myself that today, I have privileges granting me access to explore my intuitive abilities more safely than many of my ancestors. I now see my fear, uncertainty, and distrust in my intuition resulting from hundreds of years of erasure and violence toward those who decide to reclaim a spiritual path that centers relationship with the earth, intuition, healing, and magic.

Perhaps you have a fearful one within you, trying to protect you from the pain they experienced or witnessed being inflected upon those they love for honoring their intuitive abilities. Perhaps your story involves being stolen from your land or experiencing forced assimilation, cultural erasure, violence, witch burnings, or something else. Whatever your path and history, it is likely that, at some point, there has been an intentional severance from your intuitive abilities. Learning what it is, tending to any grief it may present, honoring it, and releasing it can be a deeply healing part of your magical path. It's entirely possible that severances like these could be responsible for all sorts of internal gaslighting, fear, and shame around your magical and intuitive practice. You may find that working with someone from your ancestry who's walked a similar path may be supportive as you unearth possible severances and ancestral hardships. After my initial experience of tending to this intuitive severance, I shared it with trusted mentors to help integrate the experience. Most of our intuitive severances happened in communal settings and will need to heal in community too. It has also been important for me to recognize how my ancestors and I have knowingly and unknowingly perpetuated similar intuitive severances onto other groups of historically marginalized people and to make repairs for them.

Unlike the cause of our intuitive severances, the ways they manifest within our practices will likely be similar. Intuitive severances often appear as distrust, frequent confusion, fear, or even shame around your intuitive abilities. Understanding and appropriately naming the symptoms of an intuitive severance can be helpful in better understanding and navigating your relationship with your intuition. If you're experiencing any of these issues as you tap into your intuitive abilities, I invite you to hold yourself in deep tenderness and know there is nothing wrong with you. For many of us, our intuitive abilities have been intentionally and often violently severed from us and our people. Repairing any severances that have kept you from your intuitive abilities may be a long process because, for many, the harm has spanned multiple generations. So please be gentle with yourself as you walk this path.

Tending to and healing your intuitive severances may be a back-and-forth dance that evolves over your lifetime. This has been my personal experience. Here is an inexhaustive list of ways to approach intuitive severances within yourself and your practice. As always, take what you like, leave the rest, and modify them however you'd like.

### Ways to Tend to Intuitive Severances

1.  Commit to spending consistent time engaging with intuitive energy and your intuitive abilities. Doing so will give you a baseline of your intuitive abilities in your body so you can better determine how you react to them when they arise. If you already know how your body processes intuitive energy, move to the following suggestions. If you're unsure how intuitive information shows up in your body, utilize the tips earlier in this chapter (or any other guidance you resonate with regarding connecting with intuitive energy) regularly

until you can better recognize when intuitive energy flows through you.

2.  Notice what feelings arise when you feel intuitive information surface within. Consider keeping a journal or notes on your phone to record what arises when you sense an impending intuitive nudge. Track this over a month or more, and note repetitive responses to your intuition, such as fear, shame, and distrust. As you become more aware of your automatic responses to your intuition, notice what it would feel like to replace them with curiosity, openness, or trust.

3.  Learn more about your ancestry or connect with your ancestors in the spirit realm in relation to your intuition. Notice what arises, and journal about it if you feel called. Revisit the ancestor meditation in Chapter 2 for support with this.

4.  If you're aware of what some of your intuitive severances may be, create space to tend to your grief around them. Consider giving your grief space to be witnessed and tended to through feeling your grief somatically, through breathwork, crying, journaling, or ritual. Grief tending may feel difficult in a society that often neglects grief. For me, grief tending sometimes looks like giving myself an hour or even a day of slowness to be with and tend to my feelings.

5.  Celebrate yourself when you do honor intuitive nudges and notice how it makes you feel. Honoring your intuition might not initially make you feel good, and that's okay! It can take time to fully reclaim your intuitive abilities; this includes celebrating them. Consider recording your experience in a journal and creating a celebratory ritual for yourself. Celebratory rituals for me look like giving an offering to my spiritual allies or ancestors, telling a trusted human about my experience (this can

be especially healing when it's someone I know will share my enthusiasm!), creating a special piece of art or poem to commemorate the experience, intentionally lighting a candle, or simply enjoying some time in a favorite outside space. It doesn't need to be complicated.

6. Get support! Try to connect with others, individually or communally, who might have similar ancestral wounds. Connecting with others, especially in person, can sometimes be challenging and requires vulnerability. If working individually with a mentor or teacher with a similar ancestry is accessible, that can be a supportive way to start. Finding online communities can also be deeply nourishing. As always, and especially when working with others, apply your discernment.

Intuitive information is abundant all around you. You will likely discover that your environment has a lot to share and usually really *wants* to share! In fact, you may find that as you become more comfortable exploring your intuition, it becomes automatic, and you may need to consciously choose not to engage it at certain times. Building up an intuitive language between you and the different energies you engage with can help create boundaries and deeper understanding in your intuitive interactions.

## Crafting Your Intuitive Language

There is very little within a magical practice that happens in isolation. As we'll explore in the next chapter, magic is deeply relational, and intuition is no different. In revisiting the idea of intuition being something you invoke or step into, in this section, I will encourage you to form a unique language with that intuitive magical current. Creating a form of communication that works best with your body and the unique relationship you have with intuition will add a layer of support to your intuitive foundation. It will also help you to deepen your trust in these intuitive forces.

When forming an intuitive language, it's helpful to remember that the way you interpret the world is unique to you. How you view a symbol of a heart or how you understand love may be very different for you than it is for others.

An easy place to start building an intuitive language is discerning between yes and no. I worked with one of my spiritual allies to form a yes/no system that works for us. Yours might look different. I simply ask my guide to show me a green color for yes and red for no. I've also learned to distinguish between yes and no based on how my body feels. Yes feels like an opening sensation in my body, while no feels like my body becomes heavier and broader. You might choose between two images, sensations, or something else entirely to differentiate between yes and no. I've used this communication system in countless ways, with my guide and beyond. Some examples include deciding which plants to collaborate with in a spell, working with energy clients to help me determine the best course of action for them, finding my way through a forest off-trail, and determining whether or not to engage with someone. There are endless ways to rely on an intuitive yes/no system. After practicing for a while, you'll likely find that it becomes second nature, and you might not even realize you're doing it.

Beyond a simple yes/no system, you might also find it helpful to decide upon standard symbols, sounds, or feelings to help you communicate within the realm of intuition. I often hear this sort of psychic communication discussed in mediumship. Again, I want to stress the value of creating a means of intuitive communication within your magical practice, especially when crafting your own magic. Expanding your communication beyond a simple yes/no system will make it so much easier for you to engage with the land you're on, your ancestors, and the different energies you decide to collaborate with in your magic-making process. I truly believe that this is the way many of our ancestors, and many Indigenous folks today, move or moved through the world regularly. This is where the remembrance comes in for me, and may for you as well. When I cultivate the ability to communicate with intuitive currents all around me and trust it, it feels both natural and healing.

Forming a more expansive intuitive language beyond a yes/no system may take time. It certainly has for me. Practicing working with intuition often and in different settings has been key to forming a language that works for me. By practicing often, you will likely see patterns emerge and notice that you see, feel, or hear specific things regarding certain topics. As you begin developing deeper relationships with your spirit team (allies, guides, and ancestors), you will be able to work alongside them to help create your intuitive language as well. For example, you could ask a guide to show you a specific image or imprint a feeling in your body to represent danger, safety, wisdom, or love. You might also correlate specific signs or sensations with guides trying to get your attention. Your intuitive language will be unique to you, which is another reason why it's so important to be an active participant in cultivating it. I'm often approached by folks who ask me questions like, "I saw a hawk in my dream. What does that mean?" I know what the hawk means to me. One of my ancestors gets my attention by showing me hawks, but that's not what the hawk represents for everyone. There may be times when you do seek outside help or even perform a simple Internet search, but don't forget to tune in to your inner wisdom keepers and unique connection to intuition. You'd be doing yourself a disservice not to.

Of course, much of what I'm sharing here is easier said than done! We live in a world that encourages us to remain focused outside of our bodies rather than in them, and many of us have deep-seated intuitive severances within us and our ancestral lineages. I want to stress again that this path is not always easy and may be harder for some than others. But learning how to form a personal relationship with your intuition to craft a magical practice of your own is deeply freeing. You will probably make mistakes along the way. I certainly have. I've misinterpreted intuitive information for myself and others, been confused, and sometimes felt disconnected. These are all normal and natural parts of building up your intuitive language. The mistakes and disconnections you experience are all powerful points of growth that will lend themselves to your unique intuitive language. The intuitive language you form will be helpful but is not the only tool in your intuitive practice. Let's explore the roles of discernment and trust in your intuitive and magical practice.

## Discernment and Expanding Your Intuitive Trust

There will be times in your magical practice when you are confused or get things wrong. These are normal parts of having a magical practice because you are human. I'd argue that more than any other field (maybe excluding surgeons), intuitives and psychics are expected to be 100 percent correct 100 percent of the time. Otherwise, they're obviously a scam, right? Of course, there are situations of dishonesty and abuse amid professional psychics and mediums, but this is true of any field. Just because a psychic, medium, healer, or magic practitioner gets something wrong does not mean that everything they say is wrong. Implying otherwise would be a ridiculous and impossible standard. If you're starting or deepening your spiritual path and think everything you interpret or that others interpret is going to be 100 percent accurate all of the time, you will be disappointed. Understanding your humanness within your magical practice is one of the gifts of having a magical practice. When I approach my intuition with curiosity, trust, *and* discernment, I leave more room for possibility. I leave more room for magic to unfold. Humans love to put things into binary categories—right/wrong, good/bad, etc. Perhaps intuition, a wildly variable and elusive energy, shouldn't be confined by our human binaries. When you sit with the discomfort of not knowing something the moment you want to, intuitive energy has the space it needs to weave more whole concepts into your heart, mind, and soul.

I often see having functioning intuitive abilities painted as something that has the power to make everything in life easy and painless. Or we're told that if you trust your intuition it will always feel good. Sure, this happens sometimes, but I've also found living my life in alignment with my intuitive abilities to be quite difficult at times. Discerning intuitive information is sometimes confusing, and determining how to act on it can be uncomfortable. There will be times when sharing intuitive information with someone could cause more harm than good. In other situations, you might have a deep intuitive knowing of something you must do even though you know it will be difficult or cause conflict. When acting on intuitive information, especially involving others, I allow myself space and patience before taking action. If action is required, and I suspect it will be uncomfortable, that's where your energetic allies and guides can help. We'll explore this more in the next chapter.

Some spiritual and magical circles frown upon anything that feels slightly uncomfortable. An unwillingness to entertain, discuss, or participate in topics that are uncomfortable is called toxic positivity, and in the spiritual community, it is called spiritual bypassing. There's nothing wrong with being a positive person, but when protecting your positivity negatively affects other humans, animals, and the environment, is it really positive? When I refuse to sit with an uncomfortable intuitive nudge, I'm not only doing myself a disservice, but I'm likely harming others as well. Think of a time when you did something you knew you needed to do but also knew it would be difficult. What positive outcomes did you experience as a result? I also want to point out that I'm not talking about negative experiences that have been inflicted upon you. That is different. Not all harms have positive outcomes. It's within the more difficult and uncomfortable parts of working alongside intuition that your ability to trust and discern will be invaluable.

Even if the intuitive information you receive doesn't make you uncomfortable, running it through various filters of discernment is the responsible thing to do. Having discernment in your intuitive practice means you can hold multiple perspectives and truths while you decide the best course of action for you, those nearest you, *and* the collective, including the plant and animal world. If your discernment doesn't include the inherent systems of oppression baked into most of our everyday lives, then it is likely that you will cause harm, even if you're utilizing your intuitive abilities. Similarly, just because you intuit something doesn't necessarily mean it's benevolent. Similar to how you have well and unwell ancestors, there may be intuitive information you come in contact with that does not have your or others' best interests at heart. This, combined with our human lenses, which have lived within a litany of oppressive systems that harm us all to varying degrees, makes a strong case for having robust discernment as you engage your intuitive abilities.

It is not difficult to see examples of how intuitive information has been used to cause harm due to misinterpretation. Think about the many wars that have been caused in the name of religion, which oftentimes began due to someone claiming they received a message about what is best for all of us. Your ability to appropriately discern the intuitive information that you interpret before you share it or act on it can save lives. This brings me to what I like to call "the discernment pie."

Part of the discomfort of living in alignment with your intuitive abilities can stem from the time it often requires to pause, reflect, and discern before taking action. Pausing rather than acting immediately gives you time to run intuitive information you receive through your personal pie of discernment. Like any good pie, having good discernment will require various ingredients or ways that you discern. My discernment pie has changed over the years, and yours likely will too. For example, as a recovering spiritual bypasser, I once believed that if something didn't feel good it wasn't true. I have since adjusted that belief. At the moment, my discernment pie includes running intuitive information through these various lenses:

**Discernment Pie Example**

This is an example of my current discernment pie. It is fluid, has changed over time, and will continue to change. Yours will likely differ from mine.

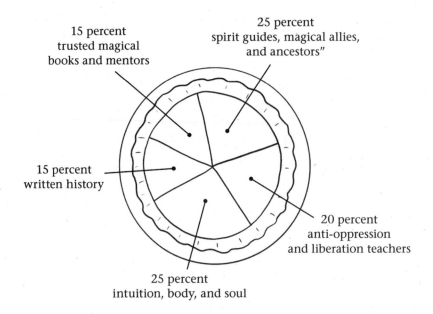

15 percent
trusted magical
books and mentors

25 percent
spirit guides, magical allies,
and ancestors"

15 percent
written history

20 percent
anti-oppression
and liberation teachers

25 percent
intuition, body, and soul

Most intuitive nudges don't require me to run through the entirety of my discernment pie, but sometimes it does. Asking for sage advice from trusted humans (or even animals and plants) will be necessary and helpful at times, but it is just one piece. Other times, going within for more perspective is what is needed. One thing discernment doesn't mean is running to every person you know, explaining your situation, and asking what they think you should do. There is undeniably a fine line between discernment and outsourcing your intuition. Reclaiming your intuitive ability all while applying your ethical framework and discernment is an entangled process that will likely include missteps and redirection. It will require a lot of trust. Like your intuitive abilities, your ability to trust them will also require practice. But trust is a muscle. The more you practice trusting your intuitive abilities, the easier it will become to lean in to them.

When I knew it was time for me to end my long-time business Zenned Out, which was a huge income source for my family, I knew that parts of it were going to be incredibly uncomfortable and confusing. I had to trust that my family and I would be provided for and that I would know how to navigate the impending death of my business and the birth of a new one. My practice of discernment showed me that all facets of cultural appropriation not only needed to go, but that I would need to remain steadfast in seeking out and uprooting future harms when they inevitably cropped up again in my practice and business. I learned from gracious teachers like Thérèse Cator, Constanza Eliana, and Dra. Rocío Rosales Meza and authors like Layla Saad, Rachel Ricketts, and Asha Frost how insidious and sneaky white supremacy and a colonizer mindset are. Because of them, I understood that I could not rely solely on my intuitive abilities to root out cultural appropriation and other harms. There would come times when my discernment would require me to reach out to others on a similar journey, and I would need to remain committed to my unlearning. I had ideas of what my future business might look like, but I certainly didn't know all the details.

I had to trust that the same intuitive nudge that called me to end that business would continue to nudge and inspire me throughout the death process and the birth of building something new. There were parts of the process when I didn't listen to the intuitive nudges I received—usually because I was rushing—and as a result, those instances were more painful than they needed to be. But when I sat in the discomfort of not knowing what my next step was, inevitably, a pathway would open. I leaned heavily on my magical practice to help me along the way by honoring necessary endings and beginnings with ritual, connecting regularly with trusted spirit guides and allies, giving offerings to the earth to show my gratitude for support and guidance, employing candle spells when I felt stuck, and reaching out to trusted friends and mentors when I needed additional help. These are some ways your magical practice can support you during transformations when you might not know what's on the other side. Even though it was hard, I knew what I needed to do—my intuition and ethical framework were abundantly clear. Leaning in to my magical tools through spell crafting and ritual allowed me to channel my discomfort and trust in the process. I do not walk this new phase perfectly either, but I now have a wealth of magical and mundane support to lean on as I navigate my intuition while remaining committed to my ethical framework.

There will almost always be an element of trust when collaborating with intuitive energy and your intuitive abilities. Throughout your magical practice, you will have opportunities to use your intuition in both small and significant ways. Both are valid and important. Sometimes the more significant intuitive nudges are easier to recognize, but there's also a lot of wisdom in the small opportunities. Sometimes the seemingly insignificant intuitive choices you honor compound into massive pivots in your life. Something I've noticed within my magical practice and that I share with others is that "you'll know when you know." In thinking about the times you've made a decision based on intuitive knowing, there was probably a pivotal moment or experience that made you know it was time to begin acting. Leaning in to that feeling of deep inner knowing can be helpful in expanding your trust, but it doesn't always mean you'll act accordingly, and that's okay too. A big part of my journey has been giving myself grace when I feel like I've missed a chance to act on an intuitive insight. Intuition tends to be pretty persistent, especially when it's important! The more you follow your intuitive nudges, the more familiar you'll become with what it feels like when you know that it's time to act, and what it feels like when it's not, and how to handle when you feel like you missed an opportunity.

Understanding what trust looks and feels like for you can be a beautiful part of forming your intuitive language and bolstering your intuitive foundation. Here are some more ways to begin expanding your intuitive trust:

## Ways to Expand Your Intuitive Trust

1. **Practice on the small stuff.** If building intuitive trust is new to you, start practicing on small things such as what candle color or herbs you use for a spell, what book you read next, or even where you go out to eat. Practice using your discernment pie (maybe not seeking outside advice, but everything else) for the small things too; it will help deepen your trust. Try to stay keenly aware of how you feel throughout the process of inviting intuition into these less significant situations. Consider journaling about what it felt like in your body during and after the decision-making process.

2. **Notice what trust feels like in current trusting relationships.** If you have family, chosen family, or friends whom you trust, notice how you feel when you're around them. What sensations do you experience in your body when you're vulnerable around them? Understanding what trust looks and feels like for you can help you identify and cultivate it in your intuitive practice too.

3. **Ask for opportunities to trust.** If you're struggling with opportunities to practice leaning on trust in your intuitive practice, ask your spirit guides and ancestors for more opportunities. I will add a word of warning to consider deciding how many opportunities you want or to add some parameters. Learning how to trust can be quite unpleasant at times, so be mindful of how you word this intent!

4.  **Revisit or journal about past experiences when you trusted or didn't trust the intuitive guidance you received.** You can probably recall a few instances where you either could have been more trusting of an intuitive nudge or when you trusted fully. Consider meditating or journaling on these experiences. Can you remember how you felt? Can you remember the pivotal moment when you decided to trust or not?

## Energetic Maintenance

As you practice engaging with and becoming more aware of the flow of intuitive energy within you and around you, you may  begin to notice a more pronounced sensitivity to it. Having an energetic maintenance, or energy cleansing, practice can be supportive. Most magical and spiritual practices worldwide have energy cleansing techniques aimed at maintaining your personal energy field or aura. The universality of energy maintenance practices cross-culturally speaks to their importance, and for good reason. Having good energy maintenance can make it much easier to recognize, discern, and have boundaries with intuitive information. You might already have a regular energy maintenance practice that works well for you. If you don't, you might find it supportive as you engage more intentionally with different intuitive energies. I'll share some important distinctions when it comes to energy maintenance techniques to help you find an energy maintenance practice that works for you, and tools and techniques to try. Energy clearing is an area where cultural appropriation has been more pronounced and harmful. We can see this with the prevalence and commercialization of plants like white sage and palo santo. Many Indigenous communities have spoken out about the harm caused by the commodification of these plants and the personal pain it causes them to see them bought, sold, and used by non-Indigenous people[4]. If you are unsure whether or not an energy maintenance plant, item, or practice is an open or closed practiced, I encourage you to revisit the questions on page 46 and 47 about how to identify cultural appropriation in your practice. I will also share some best practices in this section to avoid causing harm while practicing energy maintenance.

Though I use the terms *energy clearing* and *energy cleansing* because they're so common, I prefer the term *energy maintenance*. Though there are times when clearing away and removing energies are needed, a rebalancing of energies is often more realistic and helpful. For example, if you're feeling worried, you may find more support in focusing on grounding practices and connecting with the earth rather than trying to clear away your worry. If you have an imbalance that is causing your worry, like an anxiety disorder, it might require medical intervention, be it allopathic or otherwise, not a crystal. Trying to clear your worries away might just cause further frustration and discomfort. But if you're able to use your energy maintenance practice to feel supported in your worry, you might find that grounding allows you to be present with your worry until it passes. The terms *energy clearing* and *energy* cleansing also elicit an idea of purity that I find unhelpful in my practice. You are a being of the earth; pain and discomfort, whether they be physical, emotional, or spiritual, are normal parts of being human. I find that clearing away any and all "bad" feelings does more harm than good. Sometimes your discomfort might be trying to share something very important with you. I've learned the hard way to sit with, explore, and use my discernment with discomfort before jumping to trying to clear it away. Doing so helps inform my approach. Sometimes I need to use my magical tools, sometimes I need to see my doctor, and other times I need a bit of both.

Let's also revisit the distinction between energy maintenance and energy protection. They're often talked about at the same time even though they're very different things. Energy maintenance offers practices to help you stay connected to and present with your body, which can include either removing or calling in energy. Energy maintenance practices are the defensive or reactive things that address feeling disconnected from your body and intuition, whereas energetic protection practices are the offensive or proactive things you do to protect your sense of presence with your body and intuition.

The need for energy maintenance happens for various reasons. Similar to bacteria and viruses, you can "pick up" energy that isn't yours almost anywhere. In the same vein, you probably know some of the likely places you can pick up unwanted energy in your aura. For example, if I'm in a large crowd of people for an extended period of time, like an airport, I usually feel an energetic residue from it even after I'm home. Much of the energy you interact with is benign, but the more aware you become of the streams of intuitive energy all around you, the more pronounced they will likely become. For many magical folks, various energy maintenance techniques are part of a daily practice, although they don't have to be. Like most aspects of crafting your own magic, you will learn what works best for you and your unique needs.

Though I will offer you some energy maintenance practices here, if you have access to them, I invite you to explore different techniques aligned with your ancestry, which will help you avoid culturally appropriative practices. As you connect with your ancestors, you might find that they share unique energy maintenance practices directly with you. How often you need or want to practice energy maintenance will be personal too. As you adopt practices, you will likely notice when you need specific ones to access intuitive information in your body better. For example, I naturally lean toward overthinking and know that I feel my best when I make space for daily grounding practices. I also know that I sense—and, if I'm not careful, hold on to—other people's energy easily and that salt baths need to be a regular part of my practice. Over time, you will build practices into your days and weeks as a way to consistently support your connection to your intuition. Beyond feeling more embodied and in tune, I also view energy maintenance, especially with regard to crafting magic, as a way to be in right relationship with the energies and spirits I work with because it allows me to show up and interact embodied and present. Regular energy maintenance is one way to energetically prepare to engage with the magical world in a way that honors the sacredness of it.

When one of my clients wants to begin an energy clearing practice, I often encourage them to try a wide variety of techniques individually for about a week at a time, so they can get a sense of how each technique affects their energy. I've found for myself and in working with my clients that trying techniques one at a time for an extended period is informative. You may find that some techniques do very little for you while others make a world of difference. But if you're trying all of the crystals, smoke cleansing, and salt baths at the same time, it might be hard to tell how each technique makes you feel. Furthermore, and as you'll explore in the next chapter, having a relationship with the tools you decide to collaborate with in your energy maintenance practice is ideal. Working with different techniques one at a time gives you an opportunity to connect with them more deeply to form a relationship.

## Energy Maintenance Techniques

These are common energy maintenance techniques found cross-culturally. You'll notice I do not offer steps for these techniques. I do this because how you engage with them will be unique to your relationship with them and with your ancestry. If you're unsure how to proceed, I encourage you to connect directly with the item you intend to work with. For example, if you want to try smoke cleansing with rosemary, connect with the rosemary and ask for permission and guidance. If you are struggling with this, I encourage you to look back to the meditation earlier in this chapter, where we focused on making an intuitive connection with the environment. We will also explore the relationship-building aspect of having a magical practice in greater depth in the next chapter. The next best thing would be to seek out guidance from practitioners within your ancestry.

1. **Smoke** – Working with the smoke of plants and herbs is a common practice in many cultures, and you likely have plants in your kitchen that are ideal for working with smoke for energy maintenance. Each plant carries unique energy, so it's important to form a relationship with the plants you work with before utilizing them in this way. Rosemary, lavender, and mugwort are some of my preferred plants to work with that also align with my ancestry. Smoke cleansing is an area where cultural appropriation has run rampant. Many Indigenous communities have requested that non-Indigenous people stop commodifying and using white sage and palo santo, both sacred to Indigenous traditions, yet both can still be purchased in many chain stores, often with non-Indigenous people profiting. Anytime you work with plants it's important to ensure that it is not a closed practice (a practice intended for a specific community with specific steps). If it is, you would require explicit permission and training from that community to be in right relationship with the practice and plant.

2. **Minerals** – Crystals, stones, and salt fall into this category. Because minerals vary so much from region to region, it's another area of energy maintenance that will be contingent upon your ancestry and location, and another area to be aware of ethics and overextraction, especially when it comes to crystals. When working with crystals and minerals, the best way to

navigate ethics and overextraction is to only work with minerals you gather, with consent, from the earth. There are many layers to consider when purchasing minerals. Here are some considerations: Ask anyone you purchase minerals from if child labor was utilized in the mining or processing of the stones. Ask whether laborers are compensated with a living wage, and inquire about where the crystals or minerals are mined and processed. Consider researching whether a mineral is overextracted; this is common for many rare stones like Larimar and moldavite. Unfortunately, most sellers will likely not be able to answer these questions. Ensuring you're purchasing from those who can is a powerful way to support more ethical mining and processing of minerals. As far as energy maintenance goes, salt is a common mineral that's available in most places and has been used in magical practices worldwide. My preferred methods are salt baths, sprays, or sprinkling salt in specific locations. Be mindful not to pour copious amounts of salt in areas with plant life, as it will kill plants.

3. **Water** – The element of water is a masterful energy soother, especially when you feel overstimulated or are experiencing excess heat (physically or energetically). Working with water for energy maintenance can range from drinking water you've blessed or infused with a specific intention to swimming in a lake or ocean to taking a bath or shower. As always, I encourage you to connect with the water and ask for both permission and guidance before working with it in this way.

4. **Grounding** – Intentional and mindful connection with the earth is a powerful way to maintain, shift, or cleanse your energy. Studies indicate what many magical people already know—connecting with the earth can create measurable positive changes in our bodies[5]. Earth

reverence and connection is common among most magical and spiritual practices and varies in approaches. Practices could include going for walks more often, sitting on the earth, meditating outside, or visualizing a connection to the earth. With a little digging (pun intended) you can likely find practices unique to your ancestry related to connecting with the earth.

5. **Sound** – Sound and music are magical and can have profound effects on our physical and energetic bodies. Instruments such as bells, chimes, drums, gongs, and flutes are common in magical and spiritual practices worldwide to help facilitate various energy shifts. Beyond working with instruments, your ability to produce sound by singing, chanting, or even shouting can also be deeply nourishing. When experimenting with sound to shift your energy, I encourage you to be curious and open by noticing how different tones—whether they come from instruments, someone else, or you— make you feel and shift your energy.

6. **Visualization** – Visualization can be a powerful way to work with different energies or allies like tree spirits, animals, spirit guides, minerals, etc., who might not be physically accessible to you. However, not everyone can visualize in the mind. It's estimated that 4 percent of people have aphantasia, a phenomenon that prevents people from visualizing imagery in their minds[6]. If you fall into this category, consider relying on the other techniques mentioned or imagine how different energies or allies might feel, smell, or sound as you engage with them. If visualization is accessible to you, it can be a beneficial way to experience different energies when physical barriers exist. Visualizing or imagining these

different energies is a way to call in support for energetic maintenance, which is as valid as working with them in real life. For example, I work closely with tree spirits in my practice. I do not have physical access to all the trees that my ancestors did. When I feel a pull to connect with Birch for renewal and clearing, I can connect with Birch in my mind. If there are aspects of your magical practice that your ancestors utilized that you do not have access to, visualizing them is a valid option. We'll explore ways to do this in the next chapter. Furthermore, sometimes, it might just be easier to visualize. For example, sometimes as a death worker, the folks I serve can become agitated, which can stir feelings of discomfort within me. In situations like this, when I might not have access to all of my physical magical tools, I can visualize calling upon the element of water to help bring in a soothing energy of peace for me and my client.

In a world that often makes accessing a meaningful, magical practice challenging, I hope you find the gift of intuitive energy and your intuitive abilities invaluable in crafting your own magic. The wisdom gleaned from your unique relationship with intuitive energy can inform much of your magical practice if used with discernment. Your intuition can inform where you explore and from whom (human or otherwise) you learn. Each time my relationship with intuition deepens, its elusive qualities become more real, tangible, and as alive as the earth itself. May you, too, remember and reclaim your connection to the intuitive currents all around you.

CHAPTER 4

# Fire:
# Relationship

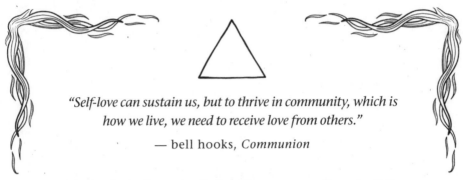

*"Self-love can sustain us, but to thrive in community, which is how we live, we need to receive love from others."*

— bell hooks, *Communion*

If magic is the art of directing energy, then building relationships with those different energies is integral to crafting your own magic. If you do not deeply understand the energy you are calling upon to work with, how will you know how to engage with it or ask it how to assist you with your magic? Of course, you can look to others; sometimes, this is necessary. But the most potent magic lies in the spark created when deep relationships are formed between you and your magical allies and spiritual guides.

When I speak to relationships, I do not mean your connection to your family, friends, or co-workers. Those are important and certainly have their place in your magical practice. Our focus in this book regarding relationships is on the relationships you hold with spirits and the energetic world around you, both seen and unseen, like trees, flowers, plants, stones, elements, the moon, the stars, Goddesses, Gods, elements, and other spiritual entities you may come across. The relational aspect of magic-making creates the initiatory spark that begins the transformational aspect of magic. Collaboration is required for fire to exist, it requires other elements, like wood and air as fuel. When you create magic, spellwork, ritual, or healing with energies you have a relationship with, a warm fire grows, enabling real transformations to spread that can be seen and felt in the physical realm. Like the lighting of a match, you now have real and tangible shifts occurring. Tangible shifts like these cannot occur in a vacuum.

Another reason I've paired the relational aspect of magic with the element of fire is that relationship-building requires an exchange of energy. Some relationships may come easier than others, but they all require a certain level of give-and-take to flourish and for deep connection and understanding to occur. For a fire to grow, there needs to be an exchange of energy. If wood is being burned, it must be dry enough; as air blows on a fire, it can either extinguish or expand it. A steady exchange of energy and information occurs for fire to exist. Fire encourages movement, action, and even getting a little uncomfortable occasionally. You can apply this to your personal relationships. Think about the very beginning of a relationship with a friend. Were there any awkward moments? Did you have to do some things that made you uncomfortable? Did it take some effort? Even if the effort was exciting and easy, I suspect there were moments of stepping outside of your comfort zone or expending some energy. A similar exchange of energy and information will need to occur as you craft your magic. Why should your magical companions and helpers receive any less?

The relationships you form in your magical practice will be unique to you, your ancestry, and where you live. Like much of what I share in this book, I cannot tell who you should form relationships with or what they might look like. Folk magic practitioner and author Gemma Gary speaks to this in her book *Traditional Witchcraft,* and states, "The day witchcraft loses regional variation is the day traditional witchcraft ceases to exist." Our practices are *intended* to vary, and much of that variation is rooted in the unique relationships we form. In this chapter, we'll explore relationship-building with the energetic and spirit world from various perspectives, including consent, connection, reciprocity, grief, shame, repairing, and how to identify your closest magical allies. Think of this chapter as the beginning of a spiral rather than a start with a finish line at the end. Akin to your human relationships, your magical relationships will constantly be in flux, always moving and changing, like fire. And, like fire, your relationships can provide much of the fuel for your magical practice.

## Why Relationships Matter in Magic

When I began my magical practice as a teenager and well into young adulthood, it was deeply rooted in extractive and appropriative practices without focusing on relationship-building or consent. The only elder I felt safe discussing my spirituality with was my grandmother, whose practice was also rooted in extraction and cultural appropriation. The books and blogs I read and many of the teachers I learned from did not speak to consent or relationship with the energetic world, not to mention that the physical world we live in revolves around extraction in the name of capitalism and constant financial gain. Naturally, one would assume that their magical practice would operate similarly. I once heard someone refer to this way of performing magic as the "spiritual vending machine," which accurately captures these sentiments.

It wasn't until I began deepening my practice with a mentor years later that she offhandedly suggested I give an offering to one of my guides. I was initially confused, as a self-proclaimed "spiritual person," yoga teacher, and magic practitioner. I thought, *Why would I need to make an offering? No one would even know, right?* As I continued sitting with the gem of wisdom my teacher handed me, I decided to try it. In that initial experience, it dawned on me that perhaps the vending machine-type magic that I'd been reading about, practicing, and sharing was not only fraught but harmful. This small mention from my mentor opened the doors to having more meaningful and powerful relationships with my spirit guides and the energetic forces I worked with. I dug deeper and discovered that my mentor's teacher was an elder practicing healing in line with her Scandinavian ancestry. I began listening to and learning from people connected to magical and spiritual practices in line with their ancestry, and I started to see a lot of overlap in practices. It seemed that nearly all earth-based magical practices were founded upon respectful relationships. Thus began one of my spiritual practice's biggest and most powerful shifts. A door opened, and I could no longer show up in my magical practice by being extractive. I needed to begin showing up as a contributing member of the web of life without expecting the allies I'd call on to assist me without forming a relationship first.

Sharing this part of my journey feels vulnerable, but I hope that by showing my humanity in this way, you can also honor yours. Understanding that extractive practices, often linked to capitalism and greed, have harmed us all can bring more compassion to this conversation. If you've neglected relationship-building and have been extractive in your magical practice, like I had been for many years, it's expected. The systems most of us have been raised in do not teach consent and reciprocity. If working relationally is new to you, feelings of guilt and shame might be present as you learn to navigate your magical practice in new ways. I invite you to lean in to self-forgiveness as you do this. I will share ways to work with these feelings later in this chapter, but I want to address that feeling them is normal! The dominant culture advocates for extraction and growth, even at the cost of harming others. Regardless of how unusual it might feel to approach a flower, stone, or tree with the same care and respect you'd approach a burgeoning friendship with a human, it is imperative when crafting your own magic. Your relationships with all beings will inform, direct, and help carry out your magic. The results of this shift in my practice were big. Over several years of forming relationships with guides, elements, and various tree and plant spirits, I now have a sense of trust and confidence in my magical practice like never before. I credit this to the fact that it's no longer just me engaging in my magical practice. Now I am in deep relationships with different energies based on consent and reciprocity.

If you believe that your magical practice can create change in the physical world, it's a safe assumption that how you craft your magic, spell, or ritual is paramount. If your intentional and relational magic-making can create positive change in the physical world, your extractive and appropriative magic will also affect the physical world, and likely not in the way you had hoped. Your actions within energetic realms have consequences. I was numb to this for a long time. If you do not fully understand the energies you're working with, do not have consent to work with them, or you misuse them, your magic-making may backfire, work against you, or harm others. The other side is that when you approach your magical practice through a relational lens, your magic will align with the energies you're working with, which improves the likelihood of having the desired result and significantly reduces the risk of causing harm.

When you work relationally, you'll likely find that your magical practice shifts from you to the collective. The very act of creating magic founded in relationship, consent, and reciprocity stitches you into a greater web, one that connects all of us. When you start working within the web of life, the allies you begin to work with regularly may start calling you in to perform magic, spells, and rituals that you didn't think you would. That's because your magical practice is no longer just about you. Working relationally doesn't mean that I don't craft magic for myself, but when I do, I am more respectful with how I engage with the various energies I work with and think about how my magic might affect others.

 Part of crafting your own magic is trusting the guidance you receive from the energetic relationships you form. When you feel the nudge to connect with a tree or a crystal, you'll be more inclined to listen. Before asking what the tree has for you, you might find yourself asking what you can do for the tree. You will form a personal community of magical allies over time and will likely see patterns in the kinds of energies you want to work with or attract. I refer to these as "magical allies," which we'll explore later in this chapter, and even more in the next chapter on correspondences. In my practice, my closest magical allies are trees and the elements. They are not the only beings I work with, but I consider them my closest magical allies. Perhaps it will be herbs, crystals, Goddesses,

fungi, water, or something else for you. Being open to working with different energies and spirits in this way will require more time and energy, but I trust you'll find the resulting relationships and magical outcomes cannot be denied.

The more relationships you form in your magical practice, the more alive the world around you becomes. I treasure the whisper from my tree allies far more than musings from a wise mentor. Don't get me wrong; having a mentor is wonderful and an important part of a magical practice, but support and guidance from your magical allies is just as valuable. As your relationships expand, you'll see the interplay between different energetic forces, how they work together, and how connected we are. Let's explore ways to start fostering a deep connection with the more-than-human and energetic world around you.

## Consent and Connection

Like any relationship you form with another human, approaching with respect and consent will serve you well. Not all beings and energies will want to connect with you; consent is essential. No hard feelings; there will be beings and energies you don't want to connect with either. Some people's practices revolve around working with various Gods and Goddesses. I work with some, but overall, it's not my thing. A pine tree also lives nearby and wants nothing to do with me. Try not to take it personally if you don't feel a deep connection with every being you come in contact with. Approaching with consent before assuming an energy or being wants to work with you will help you focus on those who *do* desire to work with you. Furthermore, honoring each plant, tree, flower, stone, or spirit as an autonomous and sovereign being will start your relationship with a baseline of respect. Beginning with respect can look like many things, depending on how you best connect with energy and spirits. If you're walking through a forest and come across a plant you desire to work with, asking aloud or within your mind is a simple way to build consent. It's for these reasons that we discussed intuition before this chapter.

Ensuring you understand how you receive psychic and intuitive information will be an important part of asking for consent. If you're clairaudient, you may hear "yes" in your mind or aloud. If you're claircognizant, you may experience an inner knowing of whether or not to proceed. If you're clairsentient, a yes might feel like an expansive opening in your body, and a no might feel like constriction in the body.

It can be helpful to practice different forms of communication. Lean on some of the practices we explored in the previous chapter. For example, you could try a yes/no style of communication with a spirit guide. If you are unsure of whether or not you're feeling a yes or a no, you can call upon a spirit guide to show you green for yes or red for no in your mind's eye. Having multiple methods for cross-checking your intuitive abilities can be helpful. It doesn't mean you don't believe or trust your intuitive abilities. It means you're being careful to not engage with beings and energies that might not want to connect. If you've been ill, overtired, or injured, it might be harder to tune in to some intuitive abilities. Further-more, there are also times when you might want to be extremely cautious about proceeding due to safety concerns, like if you're in an unfamiliar area or engaging with an animal. Having multiple intuitive methods to ask for consent provides you and those you engage with a greater sense of trust. Try not to take it personally if you receive a no from a spirit or energy. *No* doesn't mean "never," and connecting later may be more beneficial for you and the energy you desire to work with. Here's a story that illustrates this:

During a journey to connect with the spirit of vervain, I was given clear instructions to connect physically with vervain rather than through a spiritual journey. Journey-ing is my preferred method to connect with plants, and this had never happened before, so it caught me off guard. I was initially disappointed, but after further reflection, I felt honored to receive such explicit instructions for connecting. I tried growing vervain many, many times, and it would not germinate. It crushed me. Months later, after finally accepting that I wouldn't be able to grow vervain and had probably missed my window for the year, I saw a vervain plant out of the corner of my eye while driving through a park. I stopped immediately. The ensuing connection, ritual, and magic that transpired from my in-person contact with vervain over the coming weeks was perfection. So often, the energies that desire to work with you know how they want to connect. When they do, listen—that's where the real magic lives. And if you haven't met vervain, I highly recommend it.

After countless spiritual journeys to varying plants and trees, I trusted the message I received from vervain and didn't press the matter any further. When you give the energies you desire to work with the option to instruct you on how to best connect, they will often give you very clear instructions. More often than not, it will also provide you with a more magical and informative experience to connect with its energy. Part of working relationally is being humble enough to trust the innate wisdom of each plant, animal, spirit, or energy you connect with.

One of my favorite things about working from a place of consent and connection is how accessible it is. You do not need anything to begin forming your relationship. Most of your connections can come from the comfort of your own home (excluding those vervain-like situations when you're blessed with explicit instructions!). You'll learn techniques, through meditation and physical contact, to respectfully connect with various beings, spirits, and magical allies. A wonderful part about working in this way is that it will help guide you toward your magical allies without needing to commit to purchasing physical materials or trainings. Even though it might be tempting to buy a rainbow assortment of crystals or an entire apothecary of herbs, you may find through working with different crystals and herbs on an energetic plane that you only need a handful of special items to work with at any given time. Being more thoughtful about who and what you work with, especially regarding physical materials, is better for your bank account and the environment, and further disentangles you from extractive practices.

## Ways to Connect

I've been shown again and again that the most potent magic does not happen in isolation. It happens in community, and working communally can get messy. Author Sophie Strand has said, "To be correct is to be isolated," which is just as accurate in our magical practices. It's sometimes our desire to be so firmly rooted in what being "correct" is, that we lose sight of the relationships that have the potential to teach other truths. Like me, you'll probably make mistakes, feel awkward, or feel like you're doing it all wrong sometimes. Not only is this okay, but it's also powerful. Within the humility of not always being "correct," we open ourselves to boundless possibilities. Let's explore common ways to connect with energies and spirits in ordinary and non-ordinary reality. As always, these are some techniques. You may find more techniques while experimenting or learning more about magical practices from your ancestry. Trust what you're drawn to, allow yourself to fail, and don't rely solely on my offerings.

## Energetic Connection through Meditation or Spiritual Journey

Meditation and journeying are very different, but they have a similar flavor. They can each help you engage with different energies without having a specific crystal, herb, or tree present. These are ideal methods for connecting when you do not or cannot engage with the energy of something in physical form and for determining which energies may desire to work with you. Through meditation or a spiritual journey, you are opening yourself up to experience the energetic signature or vibration of a specific energy or spirit; however, in a spiritual journey, you are connecting in a more embodied way. Approach both with care and respect, especially journeying. Let's explore some of the differences between meditation and journeying so you can determine which approach might work best for you.

One way to describe meditation is to intentionally focus on something, like your breath, body, or energy you seek to engage, while you disengage from your day-to-day thoughts. In my experience and training, the goal of meditation is not to turn off your thoughts but rather to coexist with them as you intentionally direct your focus elsewhere. Focusing your internal gaze on a specific area might include frequent opportunities to redirect your focus. This is normal. There are countless meditation techniques, some of which I'll share with you here. On the other hand, a spiritual journey can be more akin to astral travel or an out-of-body experience. In meditation, the mind is focused on the present moment while remaining in the physical body. During a spiritual journey, the mind is focused on traveling to a different energetic plane, enabling you to engage with different spiritual beings in a way that more closely resembles an embodied physical experience. One of my grand mentors (a term I coined for a mentor of one of my mentors) often reminded her students that journeys are real. Journeying is not an imagined experience; it is real.

How you experience a spiritual journey will vary based on your level of experience in journeying, how tuned in you are to your intuitive and psychic abilities, and how your unique intuitive abilities manifest. For those who identify as primarily clairvoyant (clear seeing), a spiritual journey may be experienced and visualized more prominently within the mind's eye. For those who identify as clairsentient (clear feeling), a spiritual journey may be a very embodied experience with various feelings and sensations. If you have a combination of or have honed various clair abilities, you may feel like you're going on a very real and embodied journey. I believe each experience is valid, although in my experience, more embodied journeys have the potential to be more profound and lasting.

Meditating to connect in this way can be a simpler approach when starting, especially if journeying is new to you. In my experience with journeying, more steps can be involved to reach your desired level of connection. In contrast, meditation can often happen in fewer steps. It's possible that your meditation could turn into a spiritual journey, even if it wasn't your intention, which was my introduction to journeying.

You may approach these techniques with a subject in mind that you'd like to connect with, or if you're unsure of where to start, you may decide to embark on a meditation or journey to allow an energy or a spirit to initiate a relationship with you. Opening yourself up this way and allowing something to come to you is an exciting way for Spirit to help dictate your path. It can also help cut out the guesswork if you don't know where to start. Even if you're a seasoned meditator or journeyer, you may feel renewed excitement in your practice by letting your guide or a magical ally lead rather than dictate who you connect with. Certain precautions are important whenever you open yourself to connect with different energies and spirits in this way. If energetic protection is new to you, consider revisiting some of the suggestions at the end of Chapter 2. Here are the basic steps for connecting with energy through meditation and journeying:

### Connection through Meditation

There are countless ways to engage in meditation, varying from culture to culture. If the techniques I share here do not work for you, seek out different techniques. A simple online search can provide you with many text and video tutorials. This meditation technique can help you connect with the energy of a specific plant, tree, crystal, symbol, Goddess, God, etc. There are endless possibilities.

## Meditation: Connection Experience

You'll need the following:

- 15–60 minutes
- Journal
- Optional: a timer, a glass of water or tea, food or drink for grounding post-meditation, and any tools you require for energetic protection

1. **Plan ahead.** Set aside some quiet, uninterrupted time to devote to this practice. Anywhere from 15–60 minutes is ideal. Spend some time opening up to who you'd like to connect with, or who might want to connect with you. Consider if there are any crystals, plants, animals, or deities that you've noticed more regularly; they might be a good starting place for connection.

2. **Prepare your area.** Place any items nearby that you may need, such as your journal, a timer, or a glass of water or tea. As best you can, create a space that makes you feel safe and comfortable. Consider the lighting, what you're wearing, the sounds present at the time of day you plan to engage in this activity, and anything else you can add to make your experience feel good for you. I've found that my meditation and journeying practices happen more regularly when I create an environment I want to be in.

3. **Protect your energy.** Based on the energetic protection options shared in Chapter 2 or your techniques, perform the necessary steps to ensure you're energetically protected.

4. **Begin to settle in.** Turn your attention inward, toward your breath, body, and your surroundings to begin disengaging from mundane concerns and thoughts. Notice the sound of your breath and how it feels as you inhale and exhale. Tune in to different body parts, noticing how your feet, legs, core, arms, and head feel. If things from the past or future pop into your head, consider saying something like, "I see you, and I will be able to engage with you later, but not now," and set it to the side as best you can. Internal interruptions like this may happen frequently, and it's very normal.

5. **Set an intention to connect.** You can state your intention internally or aloud. If you already know what or whom you'd like to connect with, you could say, "I'd like to connect with the energy of lavender. I am open and willing to receive any guidance or wisdom you want to share with me." If you're unsure of who or what you'd like to connect with, you could say, "I am open to connecting with a benevolent _____ (plant, crystal, tree, Goddess, ancestor, etc.) who would like to connect with me. I am open and willing to receive any guidance or wisdom you want to share with me." (Or something similar.)

6. **Breathe, be, and notice.** You may shut your eyes or keep them open with a soft gaze. As you sit, continue to focus on your breath and any sensations taking place in your body. Take your time here, as some energies can be quite subtle. You may find it helpful to imagine scaning your body to become more aware of sensations and to help you remain present.

7. **Ask for consent.** If you feel the presence of an energy coming forth, ask if it would like to connect. If it has come forth, it likely does, but building in time for consent will give the energy or spirit time to guide you on

how it would like to connect with you—i.e., during your meditation or possibly in a different way.

8. **Connect.** Once you've received consent, an intuitive connection will likely happen on its own and be dictated by the energy you connect with. You may experience a variety of sensations ranging from emotions, visuals in the mind's eye, words or statements that seem to pop into your head from outside of yourself, or bodily sensations. If it feels appropriate, you may also want to ask some questions at this time. Though, like any relationship, answering is not required by the energy you're engaging with.

9. **Incorporate gratitude and offerings.** When you feel it's time to end the meditation, thank the energy you've connected with. I also recommend asking if you can do anything for the energy as a show of gratitude. You may receive specific instructions for giving a physical offering or helping in another way. Acting on these invitations can be a powerful way to be reciprocal and deepen your relationship. For example, you might be encouraged to leave an offering of a specific food or drink at a specific location. If you are, try to honor it or ask for another option if the request is not doable.

10. **Close the meditation.** As you return to your physical space, consider writing down your experience in a journal. You may also find it helpful to have some food and drink to help ground you back into your body and physical environment.

## Connecting through Spiritual Journey

Journeying is more involved. It can take some practice or even training, but it is worth the effort if it is something you feel called to explore. Journeying is my preferred method of connection for most situations because it tends to be a more embodied and visceral experience without all the limitations of the physical world, time, and space. Rather than inviting energy into your space, journeying allows you to go beyond your location and energetically travel anywhere. Connecting with spirits and magical allies in their preferred or native location can help them to express themselves better and transfer information more clearly. That said, this technique might not be your preferred method. If you lean more heavily on clairaudience (clear hearing) you might prefer channeling, which can be easier to interpret through words, whereas journeying often relies heavily on clairsentience (clear feeling) and clairvoyance (clear seeing.)

Spiritual journeying has a rich history and diverse practices that vary culturally. A common thread of journeying across cultures is the idea of a lower, middle, and upper world. These differentiations may go by different names in different cultures. Though forms of journeying have been practiced in many cultures, it's important to note that some spiritual practices outline very specific ways to journey, including specific rituals, initiation, rhythmic drumming, or plant medicines that a specific person should use. The richness of different spiritual journey techniques exceeds the scope of this book and my practice. What I share here is based on my experience rooted in various earth-based pagan practices across Europe and Turtle Island.

In some circles, going on a spiritual journey is synonymous with plant medicine. Plant medicine is not necessary for journeying, nor is it part of my practice. Some practitioners advise against adding plants or drugs during journeying or at all. Furthermore, many plant medicine journey techniques have been harmfully commodified from Indigenous cultures. I encourage you to proceed with deep respect and a keen awareness of cultural appropriation if you explore different journeying techniques in a paid setting that includes plant medicine. Learning from and paying teachers from the culture in which the practice originates is ideal if you plan to explore techniques outside of your ancestry.

These instructions are a "bare-bones" version of journeying so you can fill in techniques related to your practice or ancestry, or use tips from other teachers. To connect with energies in this physical plane, I will cover journeying to the "middle world." Some of these steps will overlap with the meditation technique I've shared. I've included the option to listen to a steady drumbeat. Drumming is common in many cultures to help induce a trancelike state, and I find it to be a helpful addition, but of course, it is optional. Having a drum is not a necessity. Drumming tracks for spiritual journeys can be easily found through an online search—for purchase or for free. If you enjoy the journey technique I share here, I encourage you to explore other books, teachers, or my offerings and courses to deepen your journeying practice.

### Middle World Journey Experience

You'll need the following:

- 30–90 minutes
- Comfortable and quiet space
- Journal
- Optional: a timer, a glass of water or tea, food or drink for grounding post-meditation, and any tools you require for energetic protection

1. **Prepare.** Start your drum music, if using it.
2. **Arrive with meditation.** Follow steps 1–4 of the meditation technique on page 117-118. I recommend putting

more of an emphasis on energetic protection for a spiritual journey. Revisit Chapter 2 for more on this.

3. **Root into your anchor point.** An anchor point is a space you visualize in your mind's eye and physically imagine what it would feel like. It is your otherworld "home base." It can be any environment that makes you feel safe and supported. For many, this is a natural environment, but it doesn't have to be. It could be your childhood room if that is what feels coziest to you. As your anchor point materializes in your mind's eye, begin to root into the space, feeling present and connected, by noticing the temperature, smell, and visuals around you. Try to engage all your senses. Your anchor point will likely grow and change as you regularly connect with it.

4. **Invite your guides.** If spirit guides are a part of your practice, you may find that they appear in your anchor point; if not, you can invite them to join you. If you do not work with any guides, you can ask if any would like to make themselves known to you. Only proceed with new guides if it feels safe and comfortable.

5. **Begin your journey.** State your desire to meet and connect with the energy you want, or ask to be taken to an energy that wants to connect with you in the middle world. (Follow the suggested prompts in step 5 of the meditation technique on page 118 if you want guidance on how to state this.) Visualize a door appears within your anchor point. When you feel ready, walk through the door—with your guide, if they join you.

6. **Journey.** How your journey takes shape from here will be unique. You may be encouraged to walk, fly, swim, or be transported to another location instantly. As you arrive in new areas, engage your senses, noticing what the space looks, smells, feels, and sounds like. If ever you feel stuck, ask your guide or the energy you seek to

connect with how to proceed. It might feel like you've left your body, and it may not. Each journey is unique. If at any point you feel unsafe, know that you can come out of the journey and close your space. Allow the drumbeat to carry you through the experience and help you remain present in the journey.

7. **Ask for consent.** If you sense or see the presence of an energy coming forth, and it feels safe to proceed, ask if it would like to connect. If it has come forth, it likely does, but building in time for consent will give the energy or spirit time to guide you on how it would like to connect with you—i.e., during this journey or possibly in a different way.

8. **Connect.** Once you've received consent, an intuitive connection will likely happen on its own and be dictated by the energy you're connecting with. You may experience a variety of sensations ranging from emotions, visuals in the mind's eye, words or statements that seem to pop into your head from outside of yourself, or bodily sensations. While journeying it is also possible that you will be guided to travel to other places or realms. If you are, remember that you have agency and can decline or leave the journey at any time. If it feels appropriate, you may also want to ask some questions at this time. Though, like any relationship, answering is not required by the energy you're engaging with.

9. **Incorporate gratitude and offerings.** When you feel it's time to end the journey, thank the energy you've connected with. I also recommend asking if you can do anything for the energy as a show of gratitude. You may receive specific instructions for giving a physical offering or helping in another way.

10. **Come back.** When you feel ready to return, you will follow the same path back through the middle world that you entered from, and then go back through the

door and into your anchor point. Take some time to again root back into your anchor point. Thank your guide if they accompanied you.

11. **Close the journey.** As you return to your physical space, consider writing down your experience in a journal. You may also find it helpful to have some food and drink to help ground you back into your body and physical environment. If you cast a circle or called on energies to support you in energetic protection, release and thank them.

## Energetic Connection through Physical Contact

Connecting with spirits and energies that manifest in the physical world can be powerful; it is also an ideal technique for understanding your immediate surroundings. Forming physical connections with your local environment can deeply ground your practice. The land, plant, and animal world have stories to tell specific to your location, and simply being present with them can open pathways of communication and connection. Connecting physically can also be emotionally and physically draining or limiting. Some energies may not exist where you live or aren't accessible for monetary, safety, or legal reasons. Therefore, you may find it helpful to connect in ways outside of physical contact, like with meditation and journeying. Connecting physically will be especially helpful for those who are clairtangent (clear touching) and/or clairsentient (clear feeling.) If you identify with these clairs, connecting physically could feel overwhelming. In this section, you'll learn techniques to connect physically and tips to adjust to an abundance of incoming information.

Connecting physically with different beings can come with more pronounced sensations, especially when connecting in an environment where other beings exist, like a forest. You might feel more overwhelmed than usual in pleasant and unpleasant ways. Feelings of sadness, grief, and discomfort might also surface. Connecting deeply to your local land has the potential to uncover troubling and painful events. It leaves no room for spiritual bypassing, a phrase that describes the intentional act of avoiding uncomfortable topics and feelings within your spiritual practice. Yet, each precious layer of your magical practice, even the difficult ones, holds meaning. Like our bodies, the land holds memories, and the residual energy of the events that caused them can be intuitively sensed and felt long after the events happened. The energies and spirits of a place might not always be welcoming or feel good. You will likely sense deep pain and grief in some areas you connect with. Some of this pain and grief is ongoing due to the perpetuation of extractive practices, land ownership, and climate change. In a world where, in most places, land is owned and commodified, simply having access to land to connect with can be a source of pain. These are all important things to be aware of as you form physical connections in your magical practice because they might require further action. For some, this will mean taking extra steps to tend to your grief; for others, like me, it might also include a more active role in making repairs. It is no coincidence that many witches, pagans, and earth-based spiritual practitioners are also activists; when we connect deeply to the land, it becomes abundantly clear how far some have come from being in right relationship with the earth.

There are other ethical concerns to remember while connecting physically, especially when purchasing physical items and tools. When purchasing items, it can be important to know how they've been sourced and sold, which we discussed in Chapter 2 on ethics. We'll explore more on adding physical items or tools to your practice in Chapter 5. I encourage you to read that chapter before purchasing a huge supply of magical accessories.

## Connecting with Energy Physically

There are a couple of ways to approach working with energy physically. You may sit in a quiet room and hold a crystal or dried herb, connecting with a space where you already feel quite comfortable. Other times you may feel called to work with energy in its native habitat. Alternatively, for some energies like a tree or the land itself, you'll have to get out in your local environment. I'll share options for working with physical energies in the comforts of your home and out on the land.

### Physical Energetic Connection Experience

You'll need the following:

- 15–90 minutes
- The physical item you desire to connect with or have access to it in its native environment
- Journal
- Optional: a timer, a glass of water or tea, food or drink for grounding post-meditation, any tools you require for energetic protection

1. **Plan ahead.** Set aside some quiet, uninterrupted time to devote to this practice. Anywhere from 15 to 90 minutes is ideal. Less time will be required to connect from the comforts of your home. Spend some time thinking about what you'd like to connect with and ensure you have it ready or have access to it outdoors.

2. **Prepare your area.** Place items nearby that you may need, such as your journal, a timer, a glass of water or tea, and the item you're connecting with. As best you can, create a space that makes you feel safe and comfortable. If connecting outside, assess your surroundings to ensure you feel safe. Move to a new area, try the exercise at a different time if you do not, or do the best you can. Making contact in physical spaces won't always follow a perfect script!

3. **Protect your energy.** Based on the energetic protection options shared in Chapter 2 or your techniques, perform the necessary steps to ensure you're energetically protected, especially in a public space.

4. **Begin to settle in.** Connect with your breath and body to help quiet the mind and tune in to your body and surroundings. Notice the sound of your breath and how it feels as you inhale and exhale. If you're outside, take special care to tune in to the sights, sounds, scents, and textures around you. You may also prefer to keep your eyes open and gaze gently in front of you.

5. **Ask for consent.** If you're working with an item at home that you hold, begin holding it. If you're working outside, being close to it is sufficient. As you tune in, ask for consent to connect, which could sound like, "Green aventurine, I would like to connect with you. Are you open to this?" or "Flowing river, I would like to connect with your energy. May I do this here?" Using your intuitive tools, tune in for a yes or no to proceed. If you get a no, you could ask if there's another way it would prefer to connect.

6. **Connect.** All the suggestions shared in step 8 of the Meditation Connection Experience still apply here, but you also have the option to use your hands for a deeper connection. If you are particularly clairtangent or clairsentient, you may notice a lot more information

coming in. If you aren't, this will be an opportunity to practice these skills. If the item is small enough, try holding it in your left hand and right hand to see if there are different sensations for each. If the item you're working with is large, you can hover your hands over it or touch it to connect deeper. Remain tuned in to the body so you can notice any intuitive sensations that arise as you connect physically.

7. **Incorporate gratitude and offerings; then close.** Follow steps 9–10 of the Meditation Connection Experience on page 117:

As someone who feels a lot, working in this way, especially outside in public areas, can sometimes feel overwhelming and intuitively challenging. There are far more distractions outside, where there are other humans, animals, or energetic forces. You will likely sense and feel a lot more than you do in the comforts of your home. I offer this to prepare you because it can take practice to become comfortable connecting physically in public spaces. If you feel intimidated about working out in the land, try connecting physically at home a few times before venturing out. Here are some ways I help connect with larger areas of land or specific energies in a crowded location, whether it's people or other plant and animal life.

 **Intuitive Tips for Connecting Physically**

- Connect often and regularly to help build your relationship and to discern between different energies.

- Stay for a while when possible. Much of the natural world tends to move at a different pace than humans.

- Consider visualizing a protective bubble that includes you and a smaller area of land, plant, or animal to help focus and protect your energy if the area feels busy with people or other energies.

- Ask your guides to help you communicate by using the communication techniques shared in Chapter 4.

- Visit at different times of the day and year to become better acquainted with shifts and changes in the energy and environment.

- Focus on one specific energy or area at a time, for example, if connecting with a new forest, try connecting with a specific tree, plant, or body of water for the first few visits to establish a firm connection.

- Consider journeying to or meditating on physical locations or energies to gain a different perspective or to deepen your relationship differently as you continue to connect physically.

- Ask the environment where you should begin forming your connection if you're unsure of where to start.

- Consider preparing a small bag to take with you while connecting with the land. I've found this to be a helpful addition to my practice. My bag usually has various offerings such as crystals, a floral essence, matches, incense, a small rattle, and a plastic bag for collecting any trash I come across.

- Arrive with the intent to connect and receive what comes, without judgment. Try to leave any agenda to acquire specific information or materials at home, especially in the beginning.

- Leave time to properly close your practice before returning to mundane activities, and consider having some food and drink to help you root into ordinary reality.

## Other Ways to Connect

Let's explore other ways to begin or deepen your relationship with different energies. There are countless ways to begin your relationship journey, so don't worry if none of these feels like your preferred method. How you connect and relate to energy can be as varied as the earth itself. The general steps outlined in the previous exercises can apply here too, including creating an energetically safe space to work, asking for consent, ending with gratitude or an offering, and closing the space.

The suggestions below may be used as standalone techniques for a specific connection; or you may find that they pair nicely with other techniques too. For example, after an intense journey, I am often encouraged to experience an energy exchange through dance, movement, writing, or drawing. The ensuing trancelike dance or drawing that flows through me helps me absorb the experience on a deeper level. I encourage you to notice if you feel a nudge to express the energies you connect with in specific ways and honor it when it feels safe.

### Journaling, Freewriting, and Drawing

Use the writing and art-making tools that are accessible or feel most aligned for you. If writing on your phone is your best option, that is great. If you prefer to paint on paper, that's great too. Either hold an item in your hand, sit next to it, or bring something to mind that you'd like to deepen your relationship with. Notice any words or lines that want to flow onto your paper or device. Be patient and try not to judge what wants to come out.

### Somatic Practices

Bring an energy to mind that you'd like to connect with, or, if it's something small enough to hold, hold it in your hand or put it in a pocket. Consider starting with some gentle movement to warm your body. Begin to notice if any specific movements or dances want to be expressed. You may find it helpful to close your eyes as you connect. Try not to judge how these movements look or feel. You might feel quite awkward. You might find the most insight in the awkward movements that feel foreign and strange in your body. Reference Chapters 2 and 5 for more elaborate somatic exercises.

### Dreamwork

Your dream world is a powerful way to connect with different energies and can afford you freedoms that may otherwise be inaccessible. It can also take some practice. If connecting with your dreams doesn't come naturally to you, it may take several tries before you make contact. Be patient. Before bed, set an intention to connect with the desired energy. You could place it next to you as you sleep, if it's something small. I recommend having a journal or device nearby to record interactions or feelings as soon as you wake up.

### Ingestion

This technique comes with care and caution. Never consume a plant, water, or other organic material you have not confirmed to be safe. If you are unsure, do not ingest it. If you have done the appropriate research to determine that something is safe to ingest, it can be a powerful way to connect with its energy.

Many trees, herbs, and flowers can be eaten or used to make teas, infusions, or essences to experience their energies internally. To initiate a relationship, consider ingesting the item on its own or only with water to reduce unwanted influences. The technique of ingesting pairs well with others. For example, if connecting with the energy of lavender through making lavender tea, you may find it helpful to use writing, drawing, or dance to express any sensations that come up.

These invitations to connect and form relationships are by no means exhaustive. As you deepen your connection to your ancestry, you may discover other unique techniques for connection. You may also find that specific items and energies prefer that you connect with them in specific ways. Allow your relationship-building process with the energetic world to be curious and fluid.

## Identifying Your Magical Allies

Just like your relationships with humans, you will find that there are certain energies you connect with more easily or more deeply than others. You'll begin to discern who your magical allies are as you do. Determining this can be a powerful part of your magical journey, as it can shed light on how you can be of service to the web of life. Perhaps you will connect deeply with water and become an activist and protector for our planet's natural bodies of water. Maybe you'll come to find that you can understand animals with ease and can help to advocate for their needs and call upon their wisdom for your magic. Perhaps you'll learn that you can connect with a specific God or Goddess in a way that allows you to spread their wisdom to others. There are endless possibilities.

As you deepen your relationship with the world around you and your allies begin to surface, I've found humility invaluable. Don't underestimate the power of the small, unassuming, or not conventionally glamorous energies surrounding you. As the mycelium that supports a forest's decomposition and energy exchange[2], or the crucial $CO_2$ absorption that phytoplankton provides[3], some of the smallest and most unassuming entities support the bulk of life here, and their wisdom is needed. Try not to discount the wisdom of even the smallest or most unusual allies that present themselves to you.

The intuitive foundation you formed in the previous chapter will serve you well as you discover and form relationships with your allies. There are many ways to open yourself up to them, and like so much of crafting your own magic, it might feel uncomfortable at times, and you may find yourself second-guessing your experiences. This is normal. Again, many of us experience intuitive severance and were taught at young ages to turn off the intuitive mechanisms within that help us find our allies and guides. Here's a list of ways to become more attuned to who your allies may be:

 **Ways to Find Your Magical Allies**

- **Recall childhood memories:** Do you have childhood memories of talking to trees, plants, rocks, or imaginary friends? We are so open as young people, yet these connections often aren't honored, so they fade. If you're lucky enough to carry some of these memories with you today, you may be able to glean some insight from them to help you determine who your allies are. There is great wisdom in honoring your experiences as a young person and the spiritual connections you had. You may even find deep inner child healing opportunities by rekindling these memories and relationships. We all had different experiences as children, some more traumatic than others. Try not to be too hard on yourself if you do not have any memories of energetic connections.

- **Look to your hobbies and interests:** You may find that there are allies and guides who've already been walking alongside you for many years. Notice where your most treasured interests lie. Have you always had a fascination with rocks and crystals? Perhaps you've always been drawn to certain animals. Looking at your hobbies and interests through a spiritual lens can be incredibly helpful while determining your energetic allies.

- **Notice where your attention is drawn:** As you move about outside, whether in a forest, neighborhood, or city, notice where your attention is drawn. You may find it helpful to connect with your breath and body first to help you become more aware and in tune with your surroundings. Here are some questions to reflect upon as you engage: What are your eyes drawn to as you explore? What sounds stand out to you the most? What internal dialogues are happening within, and do they shift and change in different environments? Do you notice any internal sensations as you pass by different areas? If this resonates, try practicing it daily or weekly, noting any patterns you find. You may notice that you're pulled to the moss on the trees, the sounds of the birds, or how the air feels on your skin. These are all invitations to go deeper.

- **Learn about your allies:** As mentioned earlier in this chapter, how you connect with different energies can be used as exploratory tools. Before a spiritual journey or dreamwork, you may find it helpful to state that you'd like to learn more about who your allies are. As different energies present themselves, notice which ones excite you the most. Those are great starting points to deepen your relationship with different allies.

Deep healing can happen as you discover or rediscover your magical and spiritual allies. You might find they've been before you your entire life, waiting for you to notice or remember their presence. Your ability to connect with certain beings is a skill everyone has. I once had a session with a medium who commented that she loved that I also talked to plants. I remember thinking, *Doesn't everyone?* Her comment reminded me that my sensitivity to plants is something to celebrate and hone. You have magical allies that want to connect with you too, and these connections are also something to celebrate and hone. If you consider yourself a solitary practitioner, you might stop once you identify your magical allies! These connections can be a prominent guiding force and support system in your magical and mundane life. As they become that, you will have opportunities to reciprocate in kind.

## Reciprocity, Gratitude, and Offerings

Fire's transformative element comes through reciprocal exchanges of energy and information. Though much of your collaboration with your allies will include the magic you craft, it will likely need to  begin as a reciprocal exchange of energy. It would be naive and presumptuous to assume that any spirit or energy would want to craft magic without you first asking permission, forming a relationship, and being reciprocal. So many plants, stones, and animals called upon or utilized for non-magical and magical workings are extracted (often nonconsensually) and abused by humans. Approaching your relationships from a lens of reciprocity and gratitude before expecting to work together or receive insight or healing is a way to repair harm and form a connection based on being in the right relationship. Through your ability to be in reciprocal relationships with the seen and unseen worlds, you also have an opportunity to mend relationships that may have been out of balance. Before you take or ask for anything, you can begin by forming deeper relationships through connecting, listening, and giving offerings. Offerings include giving physical items (food, beverages, smoke, and flowers are common), sending positive or loving energy, crafting altars, being an activist, and more. We will explore these methods in greater detail later in this section.

Giving offerings and being reciprocal is not a one-size-fits-all from practice to practice or relationship to relationship. Navigating and deepening your relationships with the energetic world and how you are invited to be reciprocal will be just as diverse as your relationships with people. Your ancestral lineage might also influence your offerings. Similar to your human relationships, how close you feel with some beings and spirits will vary. There are likely some family or friends with whom you have a very deep relationship, while others remain on the surface. The ways you engage with different humans, depending on the depth of your relationships, vary too. For example, if a friend you met yesterday asked you to help them move, you might think twice before helping. Whereas if a dear friend with whom you have a deep relationship were moving, they probably wouldn't even need to ask; you'd be there ready to assist in any way you could. Furthermore, others around you have different relationships with these same people. All this to say that relationships vary immensely, and your relationships with your spiritual allies and other energies will be no different.

Understanding the nuance between different energies and your unique relationships with them is helpful to understand when giving offerings. As you form more relationships with the animate world, you will learn what kinds of offerings are most appreciated by various beings and spirits. Knowing when, how, or if you'll receive something in return is not required to give offerings. There will be those you give offerings to without asking for anything in return. You might just have an inner knowing that what you're offering is needed. This is how reciprocity works. There will likely be other relationships that provide you with tremendous support but ask for very little in return. If you find yourself giving offerings with the expectation that money will fall from the sky, remember, the vending machine style approach usually doesn't work and isn't kind. The offerings you give might not always make sense because those you engage with are often very different from you. Yet they are still sovereign and wise. Learning to trust their requests for offerings is part of your magical practice and an opportunity to honor the mystery of it.

As you begin collaborating, you will likely find that there are energies you prefer working with and that prefer working with you. Remember, these are not one-sided relationships; the desire to work together must go both ways. This is a normal part of relationships, and no reason to cast out certain spirits or beings that don't want to work with you as often as others. You will likely find that the allies that step forward to work with you less often will bring a special potency when they do.

There are many ways to begin your collaborative dance with your energetic allies. Most will center on similar themes associated with deepening a human relationship, like active listening. Here are some ways to deepen your relationships with your allies:

**Ways to Be Reciprocal**
**with Your Allies**

- **Non-extractive listening:** One of the easiest and often most overlooked ways to be reciprocal with energies you want to connect with or that want to connect with you is to give your time by being with them and listening. Several of the techniques I shared earlier in this chapter, such as physical connection, meditation, and journeying, are great examples too. While other times, connecting and being reciprocal might be as simple as sitting outside under a hawthorn tree simply to spend time with it. Psychotherapist Ellen Emmet speaks to the idea of "listening without an agenda" or non-extractive listening.[1] I try to hold this offering when I engage with new spirits or energies and try to be aware of any agendas I might have as I connect and listen. Listening without an agenda might involve asking open-ended questions like, "What would you like to share with me?," "How are you today?," "Would you like to tell me your story?" versus more extractive questions like, "How can you help me?" or "What can you give me?"

- **Physical offerings:** Giving physical gifts and offerings can be a beautiful and powerful way to deepen a relationship and be reciprocal. It is a powerful way to state your desire to connect more deeply. It shows the energy you want to engage with and how seriously you take the interaction. What you decide to offer can be extremely personal. Aside from not using harmful or nonbiodegradable items as offerings, there are endless options. If you want to deepen an energetic relationship, you might ask what kind of offering you could bring and suggest some of your usual go-to offerings. Some of my standard physical offerings are spring water collected from a local spring, food items, flowers, smoke, my menstrual blood, song, and dance. Many spiritual and magical practices contain common offerings. If you have access to this information, it can be helpful to research items that your ancestors or present-day practitioners give as offerings. If you do not, trust what your allies request.

- **Energetic offerings:** Sometimes physical offerings will not be accessible or appropriate. For example, while on a spiritual journey, you might want to give an offering. Sometimes an energetic offering will be the only option, and that is okay. Your energetic offerings can be just as meaningful and well-received as physical offerings. Again, there are many ways to do this, and you may find unique techniques within magical practices aligned with your lineage. Energetic offerings may look like asking the energy you're connecting with what it would like and visualizing that item appearing in your hands. It could also look like offering energetic healing from your personal energy field or visualizing yourself dancing in your mind's eye. I have a panther ally that I work with often that requests meat. Not only is it not accessible for me to purchase large hunks of meat to throw in my yard as an offering, but I wouldn't feel good about it from an ethical perspective either. In instances like this, you might visualize your offering and share it with your guide while you connect with them in a journey space. The energy and intention of the offering is still very real.

- **Altars:** Altars are a powerful tool used in many spiritual practices and have been a huge part of my practice. The ways to work with an altar vary wildly too. One way to use them is to exchange energy with different beings or allies you work with. Altars can serve as a means of energy transfer with your magical allies. When using an altar to connect more deeply with an ally, the best place to start is to ask what that ally would like on the altar. Think of your altar offering as a way to celebrate them, the relationship, and your connection. At the time of writing this, I recently created an altar for the Goddess Brigid in honor of the seasonal celebration of Imbolc. I placed items on the altar associated with her and also offered some of my energy to her by crafting Brigid's cross. Through crafting a symbol associated with Goddess Brigid, I connected with her energy more deeply and expressed my appreciation for her by spending time crafting Brigid's cross. How you work with your altars for offerings can be simple or elaborate. I invite you to start with what feels most natural and comfortable. Revisit the ancestor altar exercise in Chapter 2 for more on creating an altar.

- **Activism and protection:** Part of being in a reciprocal relationship will involve offering your help and protection when needed. Remember, the energies you connect with are not a one-sided vending machine. Sometimes rather than giving something, you might be encouraged to protect the land by removing litter, pests, or invasive species. Or to advocate for an ally at a communal or political level. These are extremely important ways to give back and deepen your relationships with your allies. They may not always be fun or glamorous, but they are important and deeply fulfilling.

Approach your offerings to the energetic and spirit realm with curiosity and respect. I also invite you to remember that the way your offerings are received and felt by the energetic realm does not need to make sense logically, and it often won't. Your food offering to a land spirit that a local squirrel might eat still has the same desired effect. In these situations, I try not to presume to understand how the magical world works and invite you to do the same.

Similar to identifying your allies, much of forming a reciprocal relationship with them will rely upon your intuitive instincts. Because of this, you will likely make mistakes and even cause harm at times. Causing harm and needing to make repairs is a normal part of deepening relationships. Like most relationships, grief, shame, and making repairs will also be part of them, even in your magical practice. And, like any close relationship, addressing possible grief and shame to make a repair is usually worth the effort it requires. The good news is usually the spirit world is far more forgiving than most humans.

## Making Space for Grief, Shame, and Repair

Your relationships with the energetic and spiritual realm will ebb and flow over time. Within the cycles of your magical relationships, opportunities to be with shame, grief, and guilt will surface. So will your need to make repairs and amends. These are all normal and healthy parts of being in a relationship. Extending them to your magical and more-than-human relationships is yet another way to bring in deeper layers of respect and reciprocity. Though experiencing these feelings is normal, staying in them won't serve you or anyone. In this section, we'll explore ways to navigate feelings of shame and guilt when they surface, discuss how to make space for grief, and look at ways to make repairs when you inevitably cause harm. It happens. You're human. You will decide when and how to sit with these themes and learn from them when they arise. It will also be up to you to decide when and if you need support. These themes can bring up deeply rooted trauma for some, especially if your ancestry includes more recent proximity to systemic violence and oppression. We all deserve healing, and that healing will look different for all. I desire that when feelings of shame, guilt, or grief arise in your relationship-building process, you will honor them and ask for help when needed.

There are many ways that death and grief will surface in your magical practice, some of which we'll discuss at different points in this book. Here we'll explore honoring grief and death in your magical relationships. Just like the loss of a loved one or a beloved pet, the loss of a beloved tree spirit, whether due to moving, disease, old age, or destruction, can be as painful. Death and grief are a part of life and will inevitably touch your magical practice in various ways. As a death worker, someone who supports death processes in everyday life and beloved pets or humans, I work intimately with themes of death and grief in my practice and with clients. Reclaiming grief and death in your magical practice allows them space to weave their wisdom. We live in a dominant culture that pretends death doesn't exist. Our cultural denial of death can also work into your magical relationships. Everything dies, even aspects of the relationships you hold, both magical and mundane. Each loss you encounter will stitch a unique experience into your magical journey. Furthermore, the earth and its inhabitants, both seen and unseen, experience loss and grief too, which you will likely sense as you form deeper connections.

Allowing time and space to honor death and grief in your magical relationships can manifest in various ways. Suppose you experience loss in a relationship, physical or nonphysical. Simply acknowledging it and allowing yourself time to sit with any emotions that might surface is a wonderful starting place. You might also conduct a ritual to honor a change or death in your magical relationships. When I moved across the country, I said good-bye to many important relationships I had made with local land spirits and conducted rituals to honor our time together. It brings me peace to reflect on those rituals and that I was able to honor the cyclical nature of our relationships. You might also feel moved to create a legacy project based on certain relationships and the eventual deaths that occur within them. For example, if you lost a beloved animal familiar you work with, you could paint a picture of them to create a lasting legacy of your connection. Or, if a guide you worked with for many years moves on, you could decide to make a regular offering to honor your time together. When you experience a loss for any reason throughout your magical relationships, I invite you to find ways to bring meaning and ritual to the experience. Doing so can bring a sense of closure and peace and deeper meaning to the relationship.

Sometimes, grief presents for reasons outside of changes in your magical relationships. Grief might arise from pain and sadness in the more-than-human world or the land due to human actions or inactions. This grief might also stir shame, guilt, or sadness within you. Part of your relationship-building might include honoring and learning from these feelings and addressing them when necessary, especially if you are a descendant of colonizers living on stolen land, as I do. In these situations, I find this reminder from Patty Krawec in *Becoming Kin* helpful, "What does it mean to live on stolen land? You may not be guilty of the act of dispossession, but it is a relationship that you have inherited."

When grief surfaces, you may have opportunities to tend to wounds and make repairs for the actions of your ancestors. It is an opportunity to bring deep healing to yourself, your ancestors, and the land. Acknowledging and transmuting these feelings might become integral to your magical practice. The layers of grief will be nuanced, layered, and deeply informed by where you live and your ancestry. For those experiencing colonization, your practice may require more extensive and supportive grief tending. Some people's magical practice might require both grief tending and a need to make repairs.

Making repairs in your magical relationships will also be unique to you, deeply personal, and will range in complexity. Again, mirroring our mundane to our magical relationships, some situations with loved ones may require a simple acknowledgment of harm caused, an apology, and an inquiry on how repairs can be made. At the same time, other amends might need to occur throughout one's life. Here's an example of a situation where I needed to quickly make repairs: Once connecting with a new forest, I decided to go off the thin animal trail and wander through the bush. Not only was this physically difficult, but also all of my intuitive alarms started going off, which felt like a tightening in the trunk of my body and a loud inner dialogue requesting that I return to the trail. It was very uncomfortable emotionally and physically, and I knew I needed to get back to the trail right away because it was clear that I was causing unnecessary physical disturbances by pushing through the bush in a new area. When I finally made my way back to the trail, I took a long pause, apologized to the spirits of the forest, and asked how I should proceed. I was immediately instructed, "Stay by the creek except when you are called to travel deeper into the forest." I followed this request and moved to the creek. When I did, I found a large trail that easily led me in and out of the forest without being so disruptive. Today I travel deeper through the forest, but only when I am called to and receive permission. When I am called to move deeper into the forest, a clear path always presents itself to me. From this experience, I've continued my repair by being more aware and respectful of how I walk through wild landscapes. I am quick to ask for permission and guidance about whether I should proceed and how, rather than assuming it is okay for me to do so.

Tending to and repairing relationships due to harms caused by you or your ancestors will be a lifelong theme and look different for everyone. You will likely find it helpful to lean on your ethical framework and ancestry when you determine what this looks like for you. You might find that some of the repairs need to occur in the mundane realms. As a European American, my repair often includes mundane acts such as wealth distribution, political engagement, and divesting from systems of oppression. But it also includes tending to my ancestral lineage and ensuring that my magical practice is not causing harm. For others repair might mean resting more and reclaiming ancestral practices. Just as the magical world affects the mundane, the mundane world affects the magical. Both are needed and important. If you're unsure where repairs might need to happen in your practice, your relationships with your guides, spirits, and more-than-human allies can offer great insight and guidance around this.

##  Examples of Making Repairs in Magical Relationships

Depending on your ancestry and location, some examples may apply more than others. I invite you to read through this list and notice which examples elicit a reaction within you. They might be invitations to explore them more deeply. As always, honor your intuitive insights and check in with your magical relationships before taking action.

- Ask for consent and permission before engaging with or taking plant material or other natural items.

- Listen and don't assume you know best while working with other spirits or energies.

- Acknowledge and name when harm has been caused.

- Ask how to do better and follow through when given suggestions.

- Learn from Indigenous land stewards for guidance on how to care for and tend to the land.

- Vote in ways that protect the land and Indigenous stewards of the land.

- Invest your time and energy in local politics and direct action supported by Indigenous land stewards.

- Find ways to disperse your wealth through mutual aid that supports the global majority, if your privilege provides you with easier access to wealth.

- Support land back movements and return the land to Indigenous hands whenever possible.

Though news cycles and social media can easily pull your attention to events across the globe, making repairs might have the biggest impact in your local environment. These invitations for repair are not a call to neglect your needs and desires; martyrdom serves no one. Navigating balance in your efforts to make repairs and be in the right relationship is a moving target. Be gentle with yourself and know that part of being in the right relationship resides in your ability to not show up perfectly and love yourself anyway.

Each relationship you form, whether physical or spiritual, weaves threads throughout your magical journey, creating your practice's beautiful and unique tapestry. There are so many energies here to be explored, witnessed, and connected with, and many of them desire your connection too, because many of them have not forgotten that we are connected. Don't forget that you too have value to bring, which is needed. Being in a human body offers many unique abilities that other beings cannot access. Though humans have caused harm, our physical bodies and minds can also be used for beauty, good, and healing in uniquely human ways. My relationships with the more-than-human world remind me of this truth often. May you honor each new invitation to connect as a sacred calling to widen your perspective of what is possible.

CHAPTER 5

# WATER:
## CORRESPONDENCES

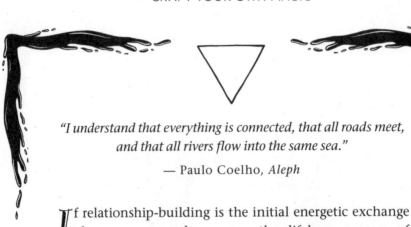

*"I understand that everything is connected, that all roads meet,
and that all rivers flow into the same sea."*

— Paulo Coelho, *Aleph*

If relationship-building is the initial energetic exchange phase, correspondences are the lifelong process of understanding how your magical relationships intertwine and interact. Correspondences teach us how to be in the community. The initial relationships you build are the spark of fire. Integrating these relationships into a larger community of correspondences is the expansive ocean. Water is our wise teacher who shows us how to be in community with different energies. As water cycles through the earth, it can shape-shift from liquid, gas, or solid as it interacts with the other elements. No element stands alone. They are consistently in community with each other, and the element of water is a potent teacher, helping us to better understand the interrelated nature of the elements and your magic. Sometimes different energies mirror, attract, amplify, neutralize, or repel, but the earth could not bring forth life without their constant dance. This chapter is an invitation to understand these interconnected relationships and how they inform your magical practice and affect the seen and unseen world around you. It is the study of correspondences.

Correspondences are energies that have an affinity for each other and can amplify, neutralize, or offset other energies in your magical workings. They are why many decide to set intentions at the new moon—a time of new beginnings reflected in the moon's cycles. There are many natural systems within and around us, such as the phases of the moon and the seasons, whose energy can serve as a foundation for understanding correspondences in your magical practice. We'll discuss some of them and how to work with them later in this chapter. If you already know and work with correspondences, I want you to leave this book with a fresh perspective on interacting with them. Here, I encourage you to experience correspondences holistically and nonlinearly. Instead of charts and lists, I'll invite you to lean in to the subtle nuance of your magical relationships and how they affect each other.

Understanding corresponding energies can assist in various areas of your magical practice, far beyond conducting magic, though conducting magic with them is helpful! Understanding correspondences can aid in amplifying, directing, and clarifying your magical workings with greater precision. They can also be worked with to expand your ability to communicate intuitively and deepen your relationship with a greater community of energy. Correspondences, like water, are not a single thing but rather an interconnected, fluid system that can shape-shift. Thinking of correspondences in this way reanimates and returns sovereignty to the energies you work alongside in your magical practice. If you practice magic by relying solely on a provided chart of correspondences without investigating how you relate to them and, perhaps more importantly, how those energies relate to you, you forego an opportunity to be in community with the energies you're calling upon for help. In this chapter, you'll learn how to create a personal community of correspondences, work within that community to enhance your magic, and deepen your relationships with the energetic world.

There are many ways to begin learning about and crafting your community of correspondences, several of which we'll explore here. I've found that the easiest way to begin this process is to have a regular relationship-building practice with different energies and spirits. When you form relationships with various energies, as outlined in Chapter 4, you will likely notice patterns in how different energies relate to other energies you already know. In this ongoing exchange of energy, you can form the foundation of a personal community of correspondences. Because correspondences form through your relationships with different energies, they will be extremely personal. However, if done with care, exploring correspondences in others' practices can also be supportive. Like so much of what I share in this book, there's nuance in crafting a personal community of correspondences.

You don't have to look hard to find several resources that outline thousands of established correspondences. Often, these resources provide little to no context around how the correspondences were formed or from where they originated, making creating personal correspondences feel like a black hole. Of these established correspondence sources, their contents may not always align with other practitioners' or your understanding of specific energies. For example, some people associate the element of air with the cardinal direction of east, while others associate it with the cardinal direction of south. Differences such as these are common and entirely expected. Neither is wrong, and both are correct to the practitioners who associate them as such. Discrepancies like this happen for various reasons, including differences in ancestral practices, the land you reside on, lived experiences, personal gnosis, and cultural norms. Yet, as I've mentioned, relying solely on others' resources can be a fraught process as it outsources your intuition and negates possible effects of systems of oppression. For example, some sources associate white with purity and black with disease, a direct and harmful example of white supremacy culture. Alternatively, some believe that roses symbolize love when they might represent psychic abilities or pleasure to another. These differences in opinion don't mean that roses do not have a specific and steady energy; it means that your relationship with the energy of a rose will be unique to you and, therefore, may vary from others. To add more nuance, it's common for personal correspondences to change throughout one's life; this has certainly been the case in my practice. Understanding the subtlety of personal relationships, correspondences, and their fluidity provides important context as you build community with different energies in your magical workings.

Here's a short story illustrating how personal correspondences can transform over time. When I was in my 20s, I loathed wintertime. I grew up in an area with a long winter season and dreaded the cold weather and seemingly endless, gray, cloudy days. I never associated winter with anything positive, and certainly not magical. I later moved to the desert. After living in the desert for several years, I began craving winter. After being away from it and connecting with the energy of winter in my practice, I understood its value on a deeper level. I eventually moved back to that area and was confronted with winter again. When I experienced the cold and dark winter season again, I learned to love and value it. From a different perspective, I now understand winter as a time to allow seasons of death, rest, and integration. Nothing about winter changed, but my relationship with it did. Now, the energy of wintertime is something I can call upon and commune with when I feel the pull to go inward and transform within my inner cauldron or if I desire to connect with the wisdom of the archetype of the crone. The wintertime has been woven into my correspondence community as a wise teacher for whom I have deep love and respect.

Had I tried to call upon the energy of wintertime before this transformation, it may have been useless but possibly damaging to my magical workings because I only had negative associations with it. This story illustrates why I would never assume to know what you should or should not use in a spell or ritual and why it's not always ideal to refer to a book for correspondences without running it through your intuition first. I do not know your associations with specific energies, nor does any book you read. If I do make correspondence suggestions to others, I do so with the caveat of checking it against your intuition.

Allowing yourself time to create a personal community of correspondences has many benefits within a magical practice; it is also a means of harm reduction. Understanding how different energies relate to one another will deepen your relationship with them and give you insight into how best to work with them. In *The Spiral Dance*, witch Starhawk explains, "The universe is a fluid, ever-changing energy pattern, not a collection of fixed and separate things. What affects one thing affects, in some way, all things: All is interwoven into the continuous fabric of being. Its warp and weft are energy, which is the essence of magic." Understanding correspondences on a personal level teaches you how to be in community with your magical relationships and is a reminder that your magic has consequences. Understanding how energies correspond in your local environment and beyond is essential to your relationship with the energetic world.

Though I encourage you to go beyond already established common correspondences as you build your community, it doesn't mean current resources are wrong. Not only are differing correspondences valid for the person who wrote them, but also you will tend to find similar threads across various resources. There is value in reading about others' understanding of correspondences, but I find the ideal scenario is combining this information with your intuitive relationship-building practice. You may already have an understanding of common correspondences. If so, that's great, and I have no doubt it will serve you well, and I still encourage you to read this chapter. There's a subtlety to working with correspondences that are often glossed over or assumed in magical texts. By taking responsibility for how you work with and combine energies, you add critical dimensions to your craft, dimensions of autonomy (for yourself and those you work with), and your unique connection with the energies you're working alongside. Rather than relying on the work of others, you step into a more mature way of crafting magic, one rooted in your intuition and magical relationships. As a seasoned practitioner, there's no longer anyone else to take the blame if your magic falls flat; it becomes your sacred task to connect with the energies you collaborated with to understand any shortfalls. But when things do go well, you'll know why. Unsurprisingly, creating a personal community of correspondences will be more time-consuming than picking up a book that outlines all of them for you, but it will also be more meaningful, powerful, and respectful to the energies you work alongside.

Understanding common correspondences, how to craft your own, and how to implement them in your magical practice with care and consent adds a layer of richness and collaboration to your magical workings, allowing you to honor the various energies around you, seen and unseen. It inserts you back into your rightful place within the web of life. From this space of interconnectedness, I'll invite you to begin your exploration of correspondences.

We'll explore the importance of elements and techniques to create your "inner circle" of correspondences, so you'll have a place to build a larger community. You'll also learn some common correspondences to try out and ways to craft your own correspondences. We'll end this chapter by dipping a toe into the process of crafting magic within your community of correspondences.

## Correspondences as a Community

Leaning in to the element of water associated with this chapter helps illuminate correspondences as a community. Water is the great connector responsible for all life, including us. Like water, correspondences teach us how our relationships weave into, connect to, and affect all other relationships. Taking it one step further, a robust web of correspondences is a gateway to communicating with the other realms and the beings that inhabit them. When I know how to communicate with a larger community of energy via correspondences it can make other areas of my magical practice, such as discerning intuition, giving offerings, and balancing energy, easier and more effective. Understanding correspondences helps conduct magic, but when viewed as a community you communicate with, it goes far beyond setting up the timing or selecting items for your magical workings.

Through my understanding of correspondences, I understand that every action I take, whether in ordinary or non-ordinary reality, will affect me and life around me. I cannot separate myself from the whole of life because I am the whole, just as you are and just as a plant is. In some magical circles, this is reflected in the Hermetic phrase, "As above, so below." A single drop of water from the ocean is still ocean. When I understand the interconnectedness of all life and my relationship with it, I can immerse myself in the ocean of energy present to deepen and strengthen my ability to co-create meaningful change through my magical practice. I can expand beyond "I" and enter into the cauldron of all life to weave new collaborative tapestries. Sandra Kynes, author of *Llewellyn's Complete Book of Correspondences,* expresses working with correspondences to "unite individuality with a larger purpose." Let's explore the elements as a foundation from the vantage point of correspondences as a community.

## The Elements as Foundation

AIR      FIRE    WATER    EARTH

The elements earth, air, fire, water, and Spirit appear across magical and spiritual practices worldwide. They are the foundation for many of these practices, including Hinduism, Buddhism, different kinds of folk magic, witchcraft, Wicca, and many Indigenous practices within the Americas, Africa, Australia, and more. Cross-culturally, these four or five elements are commonly depicted and worked within a circle. Due to the ubiquitousness of the elements and the circle, they serve as an ideal starting place. Not only are the elements extremely common, but the understanding of their essence holds similarities from culture to culture. Even though the elements and the circle are common, there is still much variety in what they represent and where they are placed in the circle by different cultures and practitioners. Your discernment and intuition will be needed, as these are not things I can decide for you. I've worked with the elements on a circle for most of my magical practice and find it remains relevant as my practice grows.

Within this framework of the elements transposed over a circle, you will still have incredible freedom to build an expansive and personal community of correspondences. Unsurprisingly, my invitation for you will be to form relationships with each element if you haven't already. If working with the elements is new, you can start by implementing any relationship-building techniques offered in the previous chapter or with the exercise below. You will have a basic understanding of the elements simply by reading this book, at least from my lens, as each chapter correlates to an element. Even if the elements are not new to you, you may find value in deepening your relationship with them on an ongoing basis. Each element has different wisdom to share as the seasons change, both in the earth and in your life. I work with each element annually as the seasons shift, but there are many ways to connect with them regularly. Here is an exercise to connect with the elements somatically:

### Embodiment Exercise to Meet the Elements

You'll need the following:

- 20–60 minutes
- Enough space to move your body as you are able
- Optional: physical representations of each element—e.g., a candle for fire, stone for earth, etc.—any energy protection items, a journal, and food or drink for grounding post-meditation

1. **Prepare your space.** Move everything out of the way to ensure you have adequate space to move your body as you are able. If you are working with physical items to represent the elements, ensure they are in a safe location where you can see them but they won't be knocked about.

2. **Spend two to three minutes connecting with your breath and body.** If moving your body intuitively feels difficult, consider playing some of your favorite music to allow yourself to warm up to moving your body.

3. **Create sacred space,** which could include any combination of the following: calling in the elements or cast a circle, burning herbs or incense, or calling in protection from your spirit guides.

4. **Start with the element that you feel called to.** If you already have an established foundation of working with the elements and cardinal directions, you may feel called to work with them in the compass shape, moving clockwise, starting in the East. I enjoy this method, but it is not necessary.

5. **Call upon each element,** as you approach it, in a way that feels good to you, which could sound like, "I invite in the element of air to move through me" or "I call upon the element of fire to move through my body." You can state something aloud or within your mind.

6. **Spend a couple of minutes pausing, breathing, and noticing** what is happening in your body after you've called upon an element.

7. **Allow your body to intuitively move** for each element you call upon, as you are able. If you feel stuck or unsure 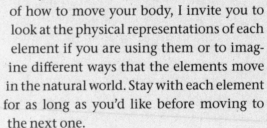 of how to move your body, I invite you to look at the physical representations of each element if you are using them or to imagine different ways that the elements move in the natural world. Stay with each element for as long as you'd like before moving to the next one.

*Loving reminder:* There is no right way to do this. It is not a performance; how your body moves does not need to look like a professional dancer. This exercise can help you connect with the elements through your body. The way your body wants to move may feel strange or unnatural, and it is normal to feel this way.

8. **Consider circling through the events a second time** or spending more time with a specific element. Proceed as you desire and are able.

9. **Thank each element** for communing with you when you are ready to close this practice.

10. **Consider having some food and drink** to ground yourself after this practice.

11. **Consider journaling** about how each element felt as you moved with it.

A variation of this exercise is to embody these elements while engaging with them physically. Some examples might be moving your body in sync with the flames of a fire, noticing the bodily sensations as the wind blows over your skin, intuitively moving your body through water, or feeling the support of the earth beneath your body. I'd encourage you to do so as opportunities arise. It's a magical way to experience the elements.

Return to the exercise above and other supportive activities that help you connect with the elements, as often as you feel called to. They are not intended to be one-time events. As you further your relationship with them, you may notice elemental energies more vividly in the world around you and within your practice. Ongoing communion with the elements can serve as a powerful foundation for crafting your inner circle and a greater community of correspondences because the elements weave throughout all life. As your relationship with the elements deepens, you will be able to begin crafting an inner circle of personal correspondences.

## Crafting Your Inner Circle of Correspondences

Our brains are built to form associations[1], and humans have formed them with the animate world since time immemorial. Some believe we can see this as early as prehistoric cave paintings in the representation of drawings of animals and hunting.[2] In our ancestors' need to procure food, they may have created these cave paintings depicting animals they ate and the act of hunting to honor and amplify their intentions for successful hunting. We continue to see evidence of the power of association in cultures worldwide in myth, religion, and magical practices. An example is how many global celebrations coincide with unique celestial events such as the new moon and full moon, the equinoxes, and the solstices. This common link indicates an understanding that certain celestial events can imbue their energy into and amplify important celebrations or ceremonies. Understanding these associations and their effects on various planes of existence is the art of working with corresponding energy. Creating an inner circle of correspondences from which to build a community of correspondences is what we'll explore here.

Imagine your inner circle of correspondences as your most intimate friendships; they are the energies you know most intimately and who you're most likely to turn to when you need support. You might already know what energies make up your inner circle. If not, consider the following questions:

- What drew you into the magical world?
- Which magical systems feel the most resonant and true to you? Something likely drew you in, such as the phases of the moon, the seasons, trees, symbols, numerology, astrology, etc.

- Have you noticed who or what you connect with most vividly in your magical practice?

Understanding where you feel the most resonance offers a possible starting point for crafting your inner correspondence circle. Your inner circle will likely be modeled from an already established system; this is fine too. Mostly, I find that my correspondences don't diverge from the work of others until I start working into the micro, with plant species, mineral types, animals, etc. When I speak of macro versus micro in relation to correspondences, in my practice, the macro would include the elements, moon phases, and seasons—essentially my inner circle of energies that I connect with. The micro includes more variety and detail, like the thousands of plant species and subspecies that abound in my local environment. When I start working into the micro, there tends to be more regional nuance in my relationship with them that might take more time to discern. Differentiating correspondences in this way is yet another way to understand and relate to them.

Familiarizing yourself with an inner circle that's meaningful to you will support and inform your community of correspondences as it grows. It can also make connecting with energies outside of your comfort zone easier. Similar to the mundane world, networking works best when you have an already established inner circle of connections to reach out to. Suppose you understand the energy of the dark moon well. In that case, you could connect with the energy of the dark moon to connect with other similar energies, like themes relating to death or the season of winter. This is similar to how you might go to a friend who enjoys making pies to learn how to make the best pastry dough. Your inner circle of correspondences creates avenues to connect with all other energies.

When crafting your inner circle, starting with a smaller set of energies is ideal. For example, the phases of the moon, times of day, elements, zodiac signs, colors, numbers, energy centers (sometimes called chakras), or seasons all make wonderful starting places, but you might think of others. Beginning with hundreds of types of crystals or species of plants could lend itself to a confusing inner circle. You would essentially be starting with the micro and working your way out to the macro or larger overarching themes of energy. It's possible this approach might appeal to you. If not, don't worry; you can lean in to all your energetic relationships as you expand your community of correspondences, which we'll get to soon. Furthermore, if you already have a correspondence system you know well and work with, that is great. The goal is to begin your inner circle or look at your current system with fresh eyes. You can apply the information I share here to your current understanding of correspondences. Part of using discernment in your magical practice is sometimes viewing your beliefs from different perspectives. If you find that something does need to change, know that change is a natural part of building relationships.

As a reference, see my inner circle of correspondences on page 161. I do not offer it to imply that it is the right or only way, but to illustrate a way to begin forming your inner circle of correspondences. The inner circle I work with is quite common within magical spaces and might be similar to a system you already know and love. My inner circle consists of the elements, cardinal directions, phases of the moon, and the seasons. These are the energies that I lean on most to understand corresponding energies, communicate with energy, discern my intuition, craft magic, and form connections with other energies. Another equally valuable and helpful inner circle of correspondences might be the elements, moon phases, and zodiac—the elements, the seasons, and the planets.

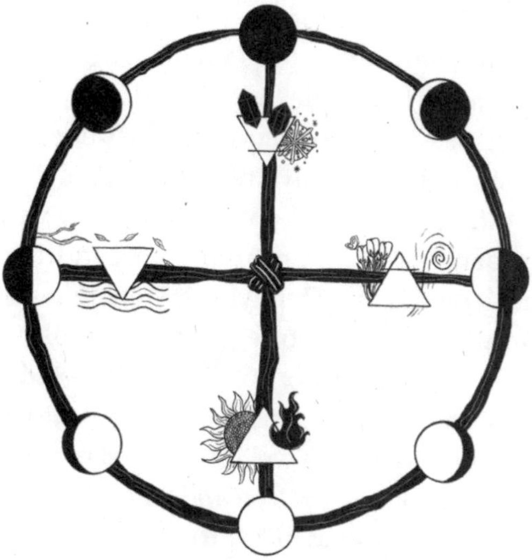

**North**
- Earth
- Dark/New moon
- Winter

**West**
- Air
- Waning crescent
- Autumn

**East**
- Air
- Waxing crescent
- Spring

**South**
- Fire
- Full moon
- Summer

## Inner Circle of Correspondences Example

Combining elements with the cardinal directions in this way is not new and is quite common among various magical and spiritual practices. Some element and cardinal direction associations vary, most notably air and fire, with fire coordinating with the East and air with the South. Both versions are correct. You might prefer viewing them as variations on a theme. Though this can feel confusing, I encourage you not to be distracted by how others craft their inner circles while you allow yours to remain adaptable. This is another excellent reason why forming relationships with the correspondences you work with is essential. Working solely from the lens of others' practices can feel confusing when you see someone else practicing differently. When your understanding of corresponding energies is based on personal relationships, you can maintain your own system while allowing someone else to have their own experience.

As you begin crafting your inner circle of correspondences, sit with each of them and run them through your discernment and intuitive abilities. Doing so can be challenging if you've already utilized a system for a long time. Astrology, for example, has a long history of established correspondences. There's no harm in keeping the correspondences you already know, but that doesn't mean you can't sit with others, inquire about their validity, and even work with correspondences that differ from yours. In my practice, this only strengthens my relationship with the energies I work with. If you are new to working with correspondences this will take time, but it will also lay the groundwork for a deeply rooted magical practice. If you are new to your magical practice, begin forming relationships with the energies you feel most called to first. As you form those relationships, you will better understand who you'd like in your inner circle of correspondences. You can begin noticing which elements correspond best. Finally, if you're new to this world, you can borrow the inner circle I work with if it resonates with you. As I said, mine is quite common; you can always change it later.

Here's an exercise to help you form or deepen your understanding of your inner circle of correspondences visually. Remember, what you come up with here doesn't need to be what you work with forever!

## Inner Circle of Correspondences Exercise

Drawing your inner circle can be a helpful way to connect with it more deeply. This exercise is easily adaptable. Modify it to an art-making technique you enjoy, like collage, painting, or something digital. I find this exercise particularly helpful because it encourages you to think about how different energies relate to each other in the circle. Their proximity to each other is just as telling as their placement. Remember, this isn't about making a perfect piece of artwork, so try to leave any inner art perfectionist you're harboring out of this.

You'll need the following:

- 20–90 minutes

- Writing utensil

- Paper or journal

- Optional: paint, colored pencils, markers, collage items, or any other creative tools

1. **Draw a circle that fills most of your page and will allow space to draw and write on the inside.**

2. **Segment your circle into four quadrants by drawing an X through the center, similar to the example.** Many practitioners, including me, view this symbol as a circle with a + through the center. I suggest drawing an X for this exercise because it allows room to write and draw.

3. **Determine whether or not you want to include a quadrant for** Spirit in this exercise. If you do, you could draw a smaller circle in the center of the larger one or a larger circle around the inner circle to create an additional ring for Spirit. Many practitioners understand the element of Spirit as an all-encompassing one that holds all the other elements. Therefore, it may not need space because it is the entire circle. This is a personal choice. Do what you feel works best for you!

4. **Imagine the circle as a compass** and write each direction on your circle.

5.   **Assign an element to each direction.** As mentioned, common associations for this are north with earth, east with air or fire, south with fire or air, and west with water. Go with what feels most intuitively aligned with you, knowing you can always change it later.

6.   **Spend some time writing or drawing words,** patterns, colors, or symbols that you associate with each element in its designated space.

7.   **Determine one or two additional correspondences** you'd like to add to each quadrant that is resonant with you. Some good examples are zodiac signs, seasons, planets, colors, moon phases, numbers, tarot suits, energy centers (sometimes called chakras), or archetypes. If possible, choose a set of energies you already know well. If nothing comes to mind, you may need to form deeper relationships with an area of study listed above before completing your inner circle. If this is you, don't fret; building a strong relationship with the elements and directions alone is huge! *Note:* You have a few options if you do not know which quadrant they would like to reside in. Connect with each of the energies you've decided to add to your inner circle to help you determine where they should go. Look ahead to the common correspondences I've outlined here and use them if they feel true to you, or seek out alternative sources. Of course, whatever you decide, include your intuition in the process.

8.   **Add more words, symbols, or images in each quadrant representing the energies you added in the last step.** You might ask yourself questions like, "What color, texture, feeling, or sound does this energy elicit?" or "What other energies remind me of this energy?"

Remember, you can always change your mind and come back to this. Nothing you create here is final.

9. **Journal or look through the questions below** to examine your relationship to each of these quadrants, when you are finished.

 **Inner Circle Follow-Up Questions**

- Spend about a minute looking over each quadrant and the correspondences you added. As you do, notice how each section makes you feel. Do you notice any sensations in your body? Do any areas stir emotions, memories, or thoughts as you look at them? Consider writing down one to two sentences about how each section makes you feel.

- Consider which quadrant(s) feels the most resonant to you. Why do you think this is?

- Consider which quadrant(s) feels the most distant to you. Why do you think this is?

- Think about how the elements and the additional correspondence(s) you added relate. Do the connections between them feel strong or distant for you?

- Notice relationships between the quadrants that are adjacent to each other vs. the quadrants that are opposite each other on the circle. What do these positional relationships have to share with you? Are there some that stand out to you more than others?

- Notice any stories or narratives forming between the different quadrants as you spend time with them. If you notice any, consider writing about them.

You might find working with correspondences in a circle more applicable in crafting relational and cyclical magic. Lists can be helpful, but working within a circle allows you to see and feel how all the energies relate. The correspondences opposite each other will have a different relationship than those right next to each other. You might also notice a clockwise momentum in the circle, affecting how correspondences next to each other relate. Understanding the energy of each quadrant of your circle can translate to greater ease in communicating with the animate world. For example, when I embark on spiritual journeys, or I am working in a trance state (a liminal space between ordinary and non-ordinary reality) to give or receive energetic healing, I often receive information through feelings and images that associate with my inner circle of correspondences. My guides and my clients' guides understand that is how I will best know what they are trying to share with me. You can also utilize your community of correspondences as a form of communication, and we'll explore this more later in this chapter.

The example of the elements transposed onto a circle is one way to begin your inner circle of correspondences, but not the only way. Be curious and open as you craft your own. Perhaps working solely with the phases of the moon will serve you best. That is valid. If working with correspondences is new to you, play with the system outlined here, knowing that it is but one way to familiarize yourself with correspondences. As you become more comfortable with it, you may notice that you want to change some of the correspondences outlined here or add ones unique to your local environment or ancestry. Expanding your community of correspondences will happen organically if you continue to form relationships with the world around you. Let's look at ways to begin expanding your inner circle of correspondences into a greater community.

## Expanding Your Community of Correspondences

Having a well-established relationship with your inner circle of correspondences will be beneficial as you expand your community of magical relationships. Your relationship with your inner circle can help you navigate new relationships with different energies because you can lean on your inner circle to better communicate with new energies. For example, suppose you deeply understand the element of water. When you come across energy with a similar feel—I say "feel" because I am clairsentient, but for you it might be sight or sound—you will already know where that energy aligns in your community of correspondences. Continue to deepen your connection and understanding of the new energy by communicating directly with it, utilizing techniques offered in the previous chapter and, if desired, by reading available information about it. Your relationship with your inner circle of correspondences is a valued asset as you form new relationships.

There are endless opportunities to expand your community of correspondences. Going for a walk in your neighborhood could garner hundreds of opportunities to learn about the world around you and how all the different energies correspond within your inner circle. Questions around timing will arise anytime you plan to craft a spell or ritual, giving you opportunities to notice and form relationships with the phases of the moon, time of day, weekdays, seasons, etc. Our brains are wired to notice patterns and associations; leaning in to this propensity can be helpful as you collaborate with various energies in your magical practice. As your magical practice grows and you form more relationships with the animate world, your community of correspondences will allow you to understand how those energies relate to others you already know and work with. This will allow you to create spells and rituals in collaboration with the energies that match a personal or collective desire. Alternatively, there may be times when you call upon specific correspondences to neutralize or amplify opposing energies present. An example might be calling upon colors or crystals associated with the element of air if you feel uninspired or calling upon the strength and power of oak to assist a community experiencing vulnerability.

The illustration and text in the following section show an example of a growing community of correspondences. Many can be observed easily in the physical world, making them organic associations, although some are certainly location specific. Like the inner circle of correspondences example, I don't offer these to say that they will be true for you but to illustrate what a growing community of correspondences might look like. You might find that some fit for you while others do not; this is fine. Both our beliefs can be true, even if they differ. As your community of correspondences grows, exploring the energy of the plants, minerals, and animals in your local environment will likely differ from my correspondences due to your unique location and ancestry. Correspondences need not be a fixed system. There's wisdom in allowing your magical associations to be more fluid. It honors the variety and aliveness of the energies you collaborate with in your magical practice.

## Community of Correspondences Example

As your community expands, so does your connection to the past, present, future, and all life. Water is the sacred keeper of all of these realms. Water is life. Science is slowly catching up with the wisdom that many Indigenous cultures worldwide already know about water. Your body is mostly water, and the water that flows through your body has flowed through the womb of the earth, streams that nourished our ancestors, clouds over our cities, and the rain that fell on the dinosaurs. Your sacred vessel contains all these memories within every molecule of water. Therefore, your community of correspondences is not only a way to connect with other energies but also a way to connect more deeply with different timelines, ancestors, and yourself.

Connecting with new energies to broaden your community of correspondences is also an ideal way to get more comfortable with relying on intuition. It can be fulfilling and exciting when you understand a new, energetic relationship without depending on other resources, only to find out that what came to you is very

## North
Night • Dark moon • Winter solstice, Midwinter
• Black, white • Death, rebirth • Bear • Yew tree

## Northwest
Waning crescent • Samhain • Purple,
orange • Crone archetype • Thistle
• Crow • Reed, elder • Scorpio

## Northeast
New moon • Imbolc • White, green
• New beginnings • Child archetype
• Ewes • Moss • Birch and
rowan tree • Aquarius

## West
Sunset • Third-quarter
moon • Autumn equinox,
Mabon • Blue, orange
• Healing, letting go
• Ivy tree and Sycamore
tree • Goldenrod
• Fish • Virgo, Libra
• Suit of cups

## East
Dawn • First quarter
moon • Spring equinox,
Ostara • Yellow, pink
• Inspiration, play,
rising energy
• Ephemeral flowers
• Birds • Ash, alder tree
• Pisces, Aries
• Suit of swords

## Southwest
Waning gibbous • Lughnasadh • Gold,
brown • Harvest, celebration • Wheat
and corn • Fox • Hazel tree • Leo

## Southeast
Waxing gibbous • Beltane • Orange, red
• Passion, sexual energy • Maiden arche-
type • Flowering trees • Rabbits
• Hawthorn tree • Taurus

## South
Midday • Full moon • Summer solstice, midsummer
• Green • Power, growth, fulfillment • Mother archetype
• Oak tree • Tree leaves • Deer • Gemini, Cancer
• Suit of wands

similar to what is written in books. Sometimes this isn't the case, which can be informative for different reasons. When this happens, it might inspire you to explore why those differences exist and shed light on the cultural or environmental differences between you and what you read. When you start a new relationship with energy based on your intuitive connection versus reading about it in a book, you form a more intimate and personal connection, even if it differs from what other texts say. Think about a time you were learning a new skill. At what point did you have a deep understanding of that skill? Was it by reading about it, or was it through direct experience? Though some of us are good at gleaning information from books, and there is value in that, the route to understanding something deeply is usually through direct experience. This is why so many fields require an apprenticeship and substantial time working in a field before approval or accreditation to work in said field. Most humans learn best through direct experience.[3] The energies you seek to know will be fully actualized and understood through direct connections, dramatically enhancing your relationships and the magic you create with them. Furthermore, at some point, you will encounter energies that you might not be able to find any written information about, or you will find conflicting information. There will be times when you will have no choice but to rely on your direct connection with energy to understand it and connect it with other energies in your community of correspondences. We'll discuss navigating this in the next section.

As you continue forming relationships with even more energies in your environment and different spiritual planes, I encourage you to try various methods to get to know those energies. Several of these were discussed in the previous chapter. Doing so will help you associate new energies within your community of correspondences in a more informed way. Yes, read all the books, lore, and information you can find about new energies, but don't let them be your only means of connecting with and understanding new energies. When you feel the pull to go to the Internet or a book to seek common correspondences for a new energy you connect with, try to remind yourself to go within first. When you learn to trust your experiences this way, you'll know them to be more true than anything you could read in a book. Unhooking from extractive ways of being and honoring your inherent wisdom may be a lifelong journey. It continues to be for me.

As you begin sensing patterns, you might notice when plants, stones, animals, or symbols resonate with each other or amplify one another in unique ways. When you begin sensing these patterns, your relationship-building is working and your community of correspondences is ready to grow. It is also an invitation to become more acutely aware of how these energies affect others you work with in your magical practice. Some beings and energies have an affinity for each other, while others prefer not to work together.

You might find it helpful to begin recording or compiling the magical associations you form. For some, this may be a journal, but writing in a journal is not the only mode of compiling information. In many magical and spiritual practices, art, dance, poetry, storytelling, and song are also powerful ways of compiling and remembering information. If you feel a natural call to one of the techniques mentioned, start there. In my practice, I use a journal, but I am also very visual, so my journals include many drawings. You do not need to excel at the abovementioned techniques to utilize them to help you compile your magical experiences and associations. Even if you don't consider yourself an artist or a singer, you might find them to be powerful mediums to express your experiences and relationships with your community of magical allies.

## Crafting Personal Connections and Correspondences

Let's spiral deeper into your community of correspondences by exploring how to navigate crafting personal correspondences. Personal correspondences are relationships that may only be true for you and the energies you work with. The need to create personal correspondences will arise when you encounter energies with no written information available or when your correspondences vary vastly or even clash with those of others. This can feel especially jarring if a practitioner you look up to disagrees with your correspondences. I want you to feel confident in your ability to craft personal correspondences informed by your relationships and intuitive abilities. We'll discuss some of the sticky parts of personal correspondences that require more nuance. I'll also share questions to consider as you wander deeper into this part of understanding correspondences and how I've navigated this. Here's an experience that illustrates what crafting personal correspondences might look like.

When I returned to the Midwest after living in the desert for ten years, Sycamore was the first tree that called to me. I had yet to work with Sycamore and wasn't familiar with any magical texts referencing it. With no foundation, connecting with and incorporating Sycamore tree into my understanding of my community of correspondences required time and effort. I used practices outlined in the previous chapter, including connecting physically, journeying, and giving offerings. Eventually, a Sycamore tree invited me to tap and consume its sap, which required time and research. Through these forms of connection and reciprocity, I allowed Sycamore to show me where it fits into the community of energies I work with most closely. It has a cozy home in the northwest corner of my inner circle, embodying water and earth elements aligned with the threshold season of Samhain. Now that we have an established relationship, I know when to call upon Sycamore, and Sycamore also knows when to reach out to me. We understand and respect each other's abilities. Had I not established this relationship before engaging in magic with Sycamore, I may have called upon it in ways unsuitable for it, which could have caused harm to the Sycamore trees, me, and the magic.

The next time you are pulled to connect with a new being or energy, whether it's a tree, stone, deity, place, or otherwise, I invite you to explore the following questions. Consider leaning on these questions as you engage in different relationship-building options outlined in the previous chapter.

### Questions to Consider when Forming Personal Correspondences

- When you ask this energy what kinds of energy it associates with, what does it tell you?

- Do you have any memories associated with the energy? What are they, and how are they affecting your relationship with the energy?

- Do you have an ancestral connection with the energy? What is it, and how might it influence your relationship with the energy?

- What does the energy's appearance—physical or in your mind's eye—tell you about it? Does its appearance have an accompanying sensation that you recognize?

- What preconceived ideas do you have about the energy, if any? Are they having any effect on how you relate to the energy?

- Does this energy feel like it is outward and action-oriented or inward and reflective? Outward and action-oriented energy may align with the waxing energy of the moon and seasons. In contrast, inward or reflective energy may indicate an alignment with the waning moon and seasons.

- Does this energy resonate with a specific element of earth, air, water, fire, or spirit?

- Is there a moon phase, season, or time of day that you feel associated with this energy?

- Based on your answers to the previous questions, are there any reflections that feel more prominent to you? If so, what?

- Do you have any trusted sources to read about this energy? If so, which parts feel true to you, and which do not?

There may be times during your process when you come into conflicting information that is hard to navigate. Perhaps you have an experience with a specific stone or plant, give it a cozy home in your community of magical associations, only to read later that its commonly accepted correspondence is vastly different than what you believe to be true. Though this is uncommon, it does happen, and it can be disconcerting when it does. You might find yourself questioning your intuitive abilities, especially if it's an energy you have a special connection with. Remember that the energies you collaborate with are sovereign beings that may differ from region to region or person to person, for various reasons. For example, an Indigenous person living in the same area as I am would have a completely different relationship with the tobacco plant. Many Indigenous communities near me have a long and established relationship with this plant that I am not a part of. Therefore the way a tobacco plant may connect to me versus an Indigenous person will likely vary. Your ability to trust and discern your personal experiences about how new energies correspond within your community of correspondences is part of being in right relationship with the spirit world.

Incorporating different energies into your community of correspondences is not always a fast process. However, the more you practice this aspect of crafting your own magic, the easier it will become—easier, not faster. Crafting your magic in this way might initially feel like learning a new language. As your understanding of this new "language" evolves, you'll begin to see patterns more quickly and have a wider body of information to pull from to make associations. Just like learning a new language, you will likely experience confusion and make mistakes; this is part of it. When mishaps occur, you now have resources to navigate them.

## Working with Your Community of Correspondences

Working communally with correspondences might initially feel unnatural or strange. Intuitive Mimi Young speaks to this by comparing our modern views of magical correspondences to our relationship with consumerism and capitalism. In her blog post "Working with Correspondences as an Animist Witch," she says, "When correspondences are approached this way in our consumerist society, it's easy to relate to correspondences from an acquisition perspective, which compels a witch to buy, acquire, collect, and objectify. Yet, some of the most effective spells I have cast are using soil from my yard, salt from my pantry, or tea from my cupboards." She writes, "When we approach correspondences from the perspective of the relationship and the honoring of the spirits we wish to work with, we will learn who they are and discover their preferences."

Connecting with a community of corresponding energies opens a portal to a broader network of needs and desires beyond humans. Yet, to access this more comprehensive and creative network, you'll need to ditch the prescribed lists of correspondences and lean in to the nuance of how your magical relationships affect each other. One way to do this is to open yourself to your community of corresponding energies and ask what they want to bring forth and how you might be able to assist. Working in this way is part of that relationship-building process and is another way to be reciprocal with your magical allies. We are relational beings, and so are the energies we work with. They are not stagnant and isolated. Like you, the corresponding energies you work with are connected with the world around them, and one way that they do this is through currents of intuitive energy.

If working with correspondences more communally is new to you, here are some ways to work with them to deepen your relationship with them. The core community of energies you work alongside can inform much of your practice and how you engage with the animate world and the spirit realm. Be open to listening to your community of correspondences as your relationships deepen. You will likely find they have many magical opportunities for you to assist with. Here are some ways to engage with your community of correspondences:

- **Communicating:** Your understanding of correspondences can strongly dictate how you communicate or form a "language" between you and different energies. When you meet a new plant, stone, etc., and want to connect with it on a deeper level, first ask for consent, and once given, you can engage with its energy to learn more about it. As you receive information about the energy of this being, you can turn to your inner circle of correspondences, like the elements or the phases of the moon, to help translate the information. For example, if you are engaging with a mushroom and see a visual in your mind's eye or feel a similar energy to the waning moon, you might infer that the mushroom's energy aligns with the waning moon. From there, you can focus on a quadrant of your larger community of correspondences to narrow down and better understand the essence of this new energy you're connecting with. How you interpret this information will depend on how you process intuitive information. If you are clairvoyant, you might see a visual of a waning crescent moon, chalice, rune, or some other correspondence to help you determine more nuance about its energy. If working in this way is new to you, initially, it can feel like a game of Guess Who? but it will become more natural over time. How long this process takes depends on many things, including how much you and that energy desire to connect. For example, if you're connecting with a plant that really wants to work with you, it will likely be quite persistent in getting your attention until you know what it wants you to know.

Working with correspondences in this way expands your practice in many ways. It gives you a framework for communication, helps you better understand how energies relate to one another, and can deeply inform your practice. It is also a more loving way to engage with the animate world. My kids get impatient when we go for walks together because I love to stop to connect with plants on our walks to learn more about them in this way. You'll likely find that you connect with some energies more easily than others; this doesn't always have to do with your intuitive abilities and can have more to do with their energy. Similar to connecting with other humans, there will always be those people you feel drawn to and others you have a more challenging time connecting with and understanding. For this reason, try not to take it personally when you have difficulty connecting with new energy.

- **Balancing energy:** Being in a community with different energies and understanding how they correspond with each other is imperative for knowing how to balance energy in your magical workings. This is a huge advantage to working with correspondences in a circle; it's easier to identify which energies can be called upon to help balance others. Knowing how to balance energy is helpful in many situations, including shifting the energy of your living space, shifting your personal energy, soothing others' energy, engaging in spellwork, and more. It's not uncommon to come across energies that might desire harmonization, especially as you deepen your ability to communicate with the animate world.

As an example, let's use energy work, which is the ability to shift and change energy with one's hands. If you perform consensual energy work on a plant, animal, or person, you might intuitively tune in to their energy first to determine what's happening. Perhaps you notice that their energy feels hot and agitated, or you see a visual in your mind of fire or inflamed skin. You could associate these feelings and visuals with the element of fire. To harmonize overactive fire energy, you might turn to the adjacent element of water to soothe it or the opposite element of earth to help ground it. From there, how you decide to work with these elements for balancing would be based on your relationship with them and your unique magical abilities. This is a simple example of how you could rely on your community of correspondences to balance energy; energy work is an extensive practice that varies vastly from culture to culture. Balancing energy can be helpful in several situations. You can apply this similar mode of working with your community of correspondences to balance your own energy, or the energy of a space or a spell. Anytime you balance energy, ensuring that you have an established relationship and have asked for consent before calling upon any of your allies to assist is good practice.

Understanding how to balance or enhance specific energies with the help of your community of correspondences will also be helpful when it comes to determining the timing of your magical workings. We will explore sacred timing in the next chapter.

- **Giving offerings:** Giving offerings is yet another area where understanding correspondences can be helpful. For example, if you're planning to give an offering to one of your guides but do not take the time to understand what sort of energy your guide desires, you might end up doing more harm than good. Understanding what kind of offering your guide might want also overlaps with your ability to communicate—another reason why understanding correspondences will be helpful. Sometimes your guide might ask for something very specific, and that's great! Other times you might get a sense or a feeling of what they want, or you might not have access to the specific thing they asked for. In these situations, leaning on your community of correspondences can be helpful.

Here's an example illustrating how I work with my community of correspondences to give offerings. While building a relationship with Juniper trees, I felt called to give them an offering. All I had on me was my go-to offering of a flower essence made from Hawthorn flowers with a very expansive and sensual energy. When I asked if Juniper would like some of the essence as an offering, I received an immediate and clear "no." I opted to offer a "thank you" with a promise to come back with a more appropriate offering. I sat with Juniper for a couple more weeks before I realized it wanted an earthy and grounding offering. I'd learned that the Juniper trees I'd been working with had a very fast-acting and transformative energy. It didn't want more energy similar to the essence I offered; it wanted something more grounding. I felt into my community of correspondences for some earthier options and landed on coffee grounds. When I connected with Juniper to ask if it would like an offering of coffee grounds, I received a warm and excited "yes." Giving offerings this way is deeply fulfilling and deepens the trust in your magical relationships.

If you travel often, giving desired offerings when you engage with a new environment can be a powerful way to make repairs with the land. There have been many situations when I've been in public spaces, especially popular natural landscapes, and I have noticed that the environment feels sad, neglected, or disrespected, often due to humans. While traveling you might not always have access to a variety of offerings to give the land what it wants most. In addition to mundane acts like picking up trash, I love to work with spring water or quartz crystals for these situations because they are usually happy to be imprinted with different energies so that I can customize an offering to the area's needs. This could look like holding a quartz or a bottle of water and asking it to be infused with love and appreciation to help offset feelings of neglect. Giving offerings like this is a simple way to be reciprocal with land spirits, especially when visiting new areas.

As you deepen your relationship with your community of correspondences, you'll find more ways to be of service to your community, loved ones, yourself, and your magical guides and allies. You'll likely even notice ways to weave corresponding energies into your mundane life, like how you decorate your house or the clothes and jewelry you decide to wear. One of the gifts of expanding your network of corresponding energies is that you'll become attuned to how deeply more-than-human kin truly desire to be a part of your life.

## Crafting Magic with Correspondences

In this section, we will begin moving into crafting magic and how correspondences weave into that process. The bulk of this information will be covered in Chapter 6. Still, it feels important to discuss how your web of correspondences directly connects with the process of crafting magic, especially regarding spellwork. It's difficult to remove the interconnected nature of this work! Here's a general example of how you might begin a new spell or ritual, how different energies may affect it, and how to work alongside your community of correspondences for an optimal outcome for all involved. Even though the following information is shared in a step-by-step format, remember that magic is a cyclical and nonlinear process. We will explore this in greater depth in Chapter 6; until then, keep this in mind as you read the following steps.

- **Formulate and thoroughly understand your goal or intention:** Before you begin assessing present energies and calling upon support from your energetic allies and community of correspondences, it will be helpful to have a crystal clear idea of your intention or goal for your spell or ritual. There are several ways to clarify your intentions, including meditating, journaling, connecting with spirit guides or ancestors, or simply taking a few days to think about it.

One way I determine whether or not I have spent enough time understanding my desire is if I can clearly write out my goal or intention. Sometimes this isn't necessary, and I might think it through a few times. How much time you spend on this will often be determined by how important the spell or ritual is to you.

- **Understand present energies:** With a clear intention, it's time to reflect on the current energy cycles to ensure that you either perform your magical workings at the ideal time or include energies to offset opposing energies. The idea of working with one single energy in your magical practice is not possible. There will always be some energies at play that are out of your control. One way to begin this process is to attune yourself to present energies such as the phase of the moon, what zodiac sign the sun is in, the season, the day, or anything else important to your practice and local environment.

When assessing the energies present—i.e., moon phase, season, astrology, day, time, etc.—you don't have to focus on every layer. However, having a basic understanding of what energies are present can help you navigate calling upon the right energies for your magical workings. Though it's exciting when everything lines up and matches your intention, it's not imperative that every external cycle line up perfectly. There may be times when you need to create a ritual to support you in slowing down for an internal underworld journey during the season of spring when everything around you is screaming activity and growth. Or perhaps the moon phase doesn't support your current spell, and you don't have the time to wait. This is another reason why your magical community of correspondences can be so helpful. When an energy that is present doesn't align with your desire or the desire of those you're collaborating with, you now have relationships formed with various energies that can neutralize others that don't match your intention and amplify what you do need.

Once you know what energies are present, you can determine if it is possible to align your magical workings with a specific time or whether you'll need to work with specific energies to offset anything you don't have control over. Spending time doing this can be a helpful stepping stone toward understanding what energies might want or need to be present.

- **Turn to your inner circle of correspondences:** Once you've tuned in to all present energies, it's time to turn to your inner circle of correspondences. These are the energies that you have the deepest relationships with, and you understand their energy the best. Within your inner circle, ask which energies would most like to assist and align with your intention. You can employ any intuitive techniques you feel comfortable with to ascertain this information. Working intuitively for this purpose might include getting quiet and connecting with your body to sense intuitive information present, or working with an intuitive tool such as a pendulum, or tarot or oracle cards. You may need to sit within your inner circle and wait for a nudge, or you might need to give it some time.

Once you have determined the core energies that want to assist you with your spell or ritual, you might feel complete and ready to carry out your magic. For example, suppose you feel called to craft a spell to bring more harmony into your home. In that case, you may feel content with the element of water and the waning moon, if the moon and the element of water are within your inner circle of corresponding energies. If you feel called to incorporate more energies into magical workings, it's time to connect with your community of correspondences that extend beyond your inner circle.

- **Call in more nuance by inviting in more corresponding energies:** Exploring your community of correspondences can be ideal when your desired outcome needs to be precise or you feel intuitively guided to incorporate more energies to your spell or ritual. Suppose your spell or ritual needs a little more energy in a specific area, because it feels like something is missing. Whatever the reason, working deeper into your community of correspondences is an ideal way to layer in more energy and add more nuance to your spells and ritual work. For example, if you're working with a black candle during the last quarter moon to protect yourself from someone else's energy, you may get a sense that it's missing something or that there's an energy that wants to assist. A starting point is to notice which energies correspond with those you've already selected. For example, in my practice, I may incorporate black tourmaline, the Algiz Rune, Rowan tree, or Mugwort because they align with the theme of protection but each lend a unique energy. From here, I would ask which energy might want to support me in the candle spell.

If you're unsure which additional corresponding energies to combine into your spell, you may feel pulled to look things up online or in books. This is not an inherently bad practice, but proceed with caution. When you seek from within your community of correspondences, you know that you're working with energies you already understand and have a relationship with.

Sometimes in my magic-making practice, I know there's another energy needed for my spell or ritual, but I don't yet know what it is. When this happens, I will usually wait for it to make itself known to me and spend extra time connecting with my intuitive abilities. I often feel like a beacon, calling out to the different realms, saying, "Hello, dear ones, I need help, but I don't yet know where to turn. Are there any energies that would like to assist me?" I don't take nudges at face value and I do my due diligence to get to know them, but I'm often delighted by the energies that come through to support my magical endeavors. When energy does make itself known to me, I always take time to familiarize myself with it by using the relationship-building techniques I mentioned in the previous chapter before expecting it to engage in magic-making with me.

- **Gather your circle of energetic allies:** Once you've decided which energies you'd like to be present for your magical workings, or they've chosen you, you can circle with these energies. Taking time to connect with the energies in each magical work is an important step that is sometimes left out. When you give yourself time to be in community with the energies you're working with for a particular spell, it becomes a more communal process. You'll be able to glean insight from the energies you circle with about how they want to express themselves in the magic. None of your magic happens in a vacuum; it will always create ripples.

When you have a clear desire or intention, you can approach your inner circle of correspondences for a specific magical working like you would with dear friends. A sense of trust will already be present because it's already been established. It's within these deeply communal circles that the most powerful magic is formed. A community is more powerful than a single person. The same is true in your magical workings. My magical practice has taught me over and over again the importance of gathering and communing with the energies I'm working with to help inform and direct our magic. In doing so, I allow space for these energies to weigh in and share how they may want to be worked with and how they can best share their gifts. I might think I know best sometimes, but I'm often reminded I don't! I'm repeatedly shown how much I have to learn from the more-than-human world. The next phase of your magic is territory we'll cover next: the realm of crafting your magic.

Your inner circle of correspondences will likely remain the same, but your community of correspondences will transform over time. As magical relationships come and go, you'll learn processes that work for you to weave in new energies. Through your circle of correspondences, you'll find new ways to engage with and understand those you work alongside. Beyond adding depth to your magical practice, I hope you'll also sense the deep support that working communally in your magical practice lends.

CHAPTER 6

# SPIRIT:
## CRAFTING YOUR PERSONAL MAGIC PRACTICE

*"The way to liberation lies in using and transforming the knowledge and energy bound up in every experience."*

— Rachel Pollack, *Seventy-Eight Degrees of Wisdom*

I had many ideas for this chapter as this book unfolded; I even believed this chapter would be far easier to write than the rest. I assumed it would come through as a simple collection of means of crafting magic. However, my guides and allies that I've been in community with throughout writing this book had other plans. Of course, they didn't let me know until I was moments away from beginning this chapter. Wisely, they did not give me the time I'd require to talk myself out of their guidance or to mold it into something more palatable. So, rather than a compendium of magical instructions, my desire is that you will find something more provocative and nourishing here and that it may alchemize something within and around you that reaches far beyond the scope of what we've been taught magic is and is not. Maybe, it is time to think differently.

Magic, spellwork, and healing work was once integrated more fluidly into our daily lives. A healer, wise person, or medicine person could be sought out for physical, emotional, or spiritual healing, as well as tending to rites of passage like coming of age, birth, and death. In many of our modern lives, these practices have been lost, institutionalized, or sterilized. As you explore your magical practice, I invite you to ponder what areas of your life, community, and the earth might benefit from more magic, mystery, and spiritual workings—especially in the mundane. If you're reading this book, I suspect that, like me, you might also

see the need for magical practices to be more pervasive in your daily life. As the title of this book suggests, my desire is to guide you to craft your own magic, and I don't know what *your* magic is. If we both agree that this current phase of humanity is in need of more magic, I do hope that you will explore and practice the magic that you are called to craft, even if it looks and feels different from anything you've read about or seen. What I can do is lay out how I've learned to craft my own magic alongside the guides, allies, ancestors, more-than-human beings, and humans I walk with. Similar to the rest of this book, I am not sharing my practice to say that it is how yours should look. My desire is that, in sharing my practice with you, it provides you with an example of what a personal practice that does not adhere to any specific magical doctrine can look like. My hope is that it will inspire you to think more expansively as you craft your personal practice.

This chapter is paired with the element of Spirit. In some parts of the world, it is called ether, and in Sanskrit, Akasha. As always, choose the language that suits you and your ancestry best. You will come across reference to all the previous chapters and elements here because Spirit is the container that simultaneously holds them and animates them. It would be impossible for me to discuss Spirit without also touching upon the elements that are held within Spirit: earth, air, fire, and water. The elements, too, are communal and connected, so you will see them mentioned throughout this chapter. I often think of Spirit as the field of energy animating us all or a thread that weaves throughout the cosmos, stitching life into every crevice. Unlike the other elements, Spirit can be challenging to point to or name because it is everything. Spirit evokes the unknowable and mysterious within and outside of us. I invite you to honor the ambiguousness of Spirit throughout this chapter and as you craft your magic.

As you sit with the mystery of Spirit, you may find you and your magical practice are guided in mysterious ways that might not always make sense. Sometimes your inner callings and actions might make sense eventually, but there will likely be times when you will be left to wonder. Trusting the unknowable qualities of your practice and the element of Spirit is part of the magic. Because Spirit lives far outside of the realms of the rational and nameable, accepting the mystery that weaves throughout your practice can conjure trust in the unknowable energies that animate our existence.

In this chapter, I will guide you to think about ways to decenter yourself in your magic and reach the potential for extraordinary transformation in working like this. We will examine materials and reimagine new ways to acquire and work with them. I will invite you again to consider reclaiming and applying cycles as a framework for crafting magic. We will also explore intentional timing, magical approaches, altars, and sacred spaces.

More than any other chapter, I invite you to be curious about any rules you've learned about magic and if they serve you or this world. As you do, perhaps consider how you might lean deeper in to the mystery of Spirit and where it might want to guide you, even if the terrain is uncharted.

## An Invitation to Decenter the Self in Magic

Decentering yourself in your magical practice doesn't mean you never craft magic to care for yourself, your family, or your community. Tending to your, your family's, and your community's needs and desires can be freeing and healing, especially if you experience the effects of oppressive systems. Decentering yourself in your magical practice invites you to consult with your inner circle of magical allies before you do. Doing so helps ensure that your magic is as potent and healing as you want it to be and that it doesn't unintentionally cause harm to other beings. With this in mind, I invite you to pause for a moment and hold in your heart our beloved planet and all the plants, animals, minerals, humans, elements, and beings that reside here. As you hold the vast diversity of these beings in your heart, how do you feel humans have stewarded their well-being? What feelings, visuals, and sensations surface when you sit with the bigness of this question? Take some time to be with these considerations.

We've all had different experiences and levels of exposure to stewarding and relating with Earth. If you grew up in an Indigenous culture or with a caretaker who engaged in Earth-based spiritual practices, you would likely have a vastly different experience holding the questions above compared to someone who was raised in a dominant culture that views nonhumans as non-sovereign beings, or worse, inanimate objects to control or from which to extract. Much of this stems from hzuman exceptionalism, also called anthropocentrism, which is a belief that humans are separate from the ecosystems we live within.[1] Human exceptionalism can extend to a belief that humans and the technology we create are better suited to solve any problem, including problems related to the ecosystems in which we exist. The current dominant culture is rife with human exceptionalism. For most of us, it was ingrained at a young age—through how we treat animals, trees, plants, and the land—that humans are the smartest and best this planet has to offer. This has not always been the overarching belief. In fact, there are Indigenous cultures today that do not experience life through the lens of human exceptionalism.

Regardless of where you came from or how you grew up, it is likely that, like me, you notice a thread (or a hundred-mile-long pipeline) of many humans needing to humble themselves and to access new and creative ways to better care for themselves, this planet, and all its beings. Most of us do our best in a stew of oppressive systems, and I am no exception. But navigating new ways of being will likely require humility, especially for those like me who've had more prominent experiences with human exceptionalism.

Humility means having the ability to consider other voices, ideas, and ways of being as more valuable than your own. In your magical practice, this can look like listening to the trees, wind, or a whale before determining your next act of magic or how you enact your magic. Humility means that you don't always assume you know best. Most would agree that humans have done a less-than-stellar job of tending to our planet and its beings. Regardless of where your heart most desires to see positive change in this world, your magical practice can help. The invitation is to consider how humility in your magical practice and divesting from human exceptionalism could create a more communal and creative approach to individual and global challenges.

There are trees, like Magnolia, whose species have lived on this planet for millions of years. Magnolia trees have witnessed the rise and fall of the dinosaurs and were initially pollinated by beetles rather than bees because bees did not yet exist![2] Can you imagine the depth of wisdom coursing through a Magnolia? Magnolia is just one example; there are many. The oceans, the land, and every seed have stories to tell and knowledge to share.

The idea of decentering yourself and unhooking from human exceptionalism in your magic can extend beyond the physical world and into Spirit realms. Perhaps for you it feels more aligned to lean on the wisdom of a deity, a muse, or ancestors. I will encourage you to center your practice around various mundane and magical beings and energies that you feel called to weave into your magical practice. You and your wise animal body are a part of this earth and, therefore, also hold deep wisdom. I do not offer the invitation to decenter yourself because I think humans are inherently wrong or harmful, but some of us are being tasked with a sacred opportunity to remember how many of our ancestors and Indigenous communities today engage with the animate world.

Many Indigenous cultures today practice in ways some might label as animistic. For others, like me and perhaps you, many of our ancestors lived with similar animistic beliefs. Here are two examples of this from different parts of the world. In her book *Plants Have So Much to Give Us, All We Have to Do Is Ask*, Anishinaabe botanical teacher Mary Siisip Geniusz shares, "All things created are alive. Some of the things created by humans are combinations of many beings. But the beings whom Creator made are all alive. They are different lifeforms. . . . All of the different orders of life, all of the different species, and individuals have both physical and a Spiritual purpose. And all of the jobs are necessary if the whole of creation is to be kept in balance." In *The Path of Druidry*, Druid Penny Billington shares, "This is a core belief—that there is a magical current of energy pouring from the land that we can access, as our forebears did. And from our experience of this, we come to the belief that this interaction is vital not only for our health, but for that of the land and the three worlds." These excerpts vary, but within them lies a core belief or essence that the land is alive and that magic and balance can be found by being in relationship with it. Doing so requires humility.

What humility and decentering look like in your magical practice will be unique to you and require collaboration with your intuitive abilities and your magical allies. One of my favorite examples of how creative it can be to work in this way is Michaela Harrison and her collaborative project called Whale Whispering. Michaela communicates with humpback whales through song with a hydrophone and aquatic speaker. She then shares the messages she receives from the whales. Simply listening to these conversations between Michaela and the whales imprints my soul with insight and wisdom. Communicating with whales is not a technique in most magical texts! Yet, the work Michaela is providing through her Whale Whispering collaboration is profoundly healing and transformative for many. Working in this way can require deep trust. This is why I encourage you to focus on reclaiming and trusting your intuitive abilities in your practice. In my practice, I work intimately with trees and receive most of my queues for when and how to create magic from them. I know others who work closely with crystals, flowers, or animals. You may already know where your closest connections lie. If you don't, they will become evident as you deepen your intuitive abilities and continue forming relationships with the animate world. When you shut the door to human exceptionalism, you open yourself to a larger world of wise beings who sincerely desire to create magic with you.

### Reimagining Materials

Tools don't make a magical practice; relationships do. The lies of capitalism and perhaps a sprinkling of social media might make it feel like you need certain things to have a meaningful magical practice. You don't. My magic has become more meaningful with fewer—but more intuitively—selected tools. Being mindful of the spirits of the tools you work with can help you remember the relational nature of your magical practice. For example, when I pick up my birch broom to assist me with energy clearing, it is not only the broom but also the spirit of birch that I call upon and engage with. If something were to happen to my birch broom, I could just as easily connect with birch to assist with energy clearing without my physical broom. Physical items can be helpful and meaningful but are only sometimes necessary. Applying your ethical framework can prove helpful when you decide it's time to work with physical materials. Let's explore creative and meaningful solutions for working with various physical materials in your magical practice.

Symbolism, visualization, writing, and imagery are powerful ways to work with all kinds of energies and beings in your practice. There will be times when it is either not possible or ethical to work with certain materials. When this happens, meaningful ways exist to engage and collaborate with the materials. Suppose you feel called to work with moldavite for a spell bag, but you do not have access to it or you feel uncomfortable purchasing it because it is being depleted so rapidly. In that case, you can connect with the spirit of moldavite and ask it for guidance. If the spirit of moldavite wants to work with you, it might provide you with a symbol, word, or image to use in its place. Similar to my birch broom, if it is the spirit or essence of moldavite assisting you with your spell, it can do that even if it is not physically present. In candle magic, it is common to carve symbols and words into the candle. By doing this, you call upon various spirits or allies to add layers of energy to your candle spell. If this same practice applies to candle magic, you can successfully apply it to most forms of your magical workings. As always, if working in these ways, I encourage you to remember and utilize techniques I offered in Chapter 4 on relationships regarding consent and being reciprocal.

There will be times when you prefer, are guided to work with, or are invited to work with physical items. When that occurs, your magical ethical framework will be important in determining where and how you acquire those items and if it is appropriate for you to acquire them. It is common practice in several cultures to only work with certain magical or spiritual items after being initiated or invited to use them; this applies to many closed practices.

However, if there is a physical item you feel deeply called to work with and it is not associated with closed practice, it might be an invitation to deepen your work in a new way. By applying your ethical framework and intuitive abilities, you can determine how best to move forward. Remember, perfection is not the goal here. You are human; you won't get it right every time, and that is okay. I've learned in my practice that my guides will be extremely clear with me when it is time to start working with a new physical item. In your practice, this might look like becoming more aware of pendulums. You may notice books, blog posts, podcasts, or dreams referencing pendulums. At this point, it may feel right to connect with a trusted spirit guide, ally, or mentor to ask about working with pendulums and the best way to proceed. If a pendu- 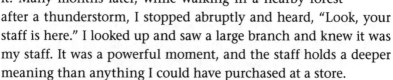 lum calls you to work together, you might receive the next steps on how to do this or be told, "Not yet." In my experience, working more intuitively with physical materials requires patience! With same-day delivery in so many areas, most of us have easy access to various magical materials, but utilizing these kinds of services may not always be best for you, your practice, or the earth. I once waited a year before acquiring a staff. My guides alerted me that it was time to work with a staff. The topic started popping up in books I was reading, and I noticed it more often. My guides told me to wait and that I would know when I saw it. Many months later, while walking in a nearby forest after a thunderstorm, I stopped abruptly and heard, "Look, your staff is here." I looked up and saw a large branch and knew it was my staff. It was a powerful moment, and the staff holds a deeper meaning than anything I could have purchased at a store.

When acquiring new materials, applying your intuitive abilities and ethical framework can be more tedious. Still, you'll likely find the extra care worth it—for your practice, those you work alongside, and the earth. When accessible, growing your own plants, foraging locally, or building relationships with local community gardens are excellent options that can simultaneously add meaning and depth to your practice. However, these options may not always be possible, and that's fine, too. The invitation here is to check in with your intuition and magical allies before incorporating anything into your magical workings, including physical materials. Sometimes, you may be guided to work with the processed cinnamon in your spice cabinet because it's what's available, and your magical allies give you a clear "yes." Knowing when and how to obtain materials won't always be so complicated. You will likely encounter times when you're outside and you become magnetized to a plant or tree that wants to work with you and invites you to take some leaves, flowers, or bark. You might embark on a guided journey when an ancestor suggests obtaining a tarot card deck or even find yourself encouraged to channel information from a group of animals. As the all-encompassing element of spirit suggests, every aspect of crafting your magic—your ancestry, ethical framework, intuitive abilities, and relationships with your community of correspondences—supports one another.

### Crafting Cyclical Magic

Like the seasons of the year and the moon's phases, you too have seasons that apply to your magical practice. Cyclical magic invites you to honor these inner and outer seasons in your magical workings. Just as living cyclically advocates not existing in a perpetual state of doing, cyclical magic reinforces a magical practice that includes phases of rest, receptiveness, integration, and intense magic-making. In the same way that wintertime helps prepare the seeds and soil for spring, phases of rest in your magical practice allow time to fully process and incorporate your magical workings. Cyclical magic can provide a supportive structure for how you engage with your practice, ultimately leading to more fruitful magic. I will lean heavily on the seasons and moon phases to express how you might apply cyclical magic to your practice. You might find that this same system works well for you or that you need to modify it. Determining what your magical patterns and cycles look like will be a personal journey,

In many witchcraft spaces and texts, it's common to read these steps: cast a circle, raise energy, perform your magic or spell, and close your circle. While these are essential parts of most magic, they neglect other vital parts of a well-rounded magical practice, like opening yourself up to and collaborating with a broader network of spirit guides, energetic allies, and time to integrate your magical workings properly. Working magic more holistically encourages you to spread the process over days, weeks, or months. Our magic was never intended to be blips of momentary events. Implying so obfuscates the depth of your magic. Your magic is intended to weave throughout your days and nights, ebbing and flowing like the moon and the tides.

When you examine the life cycle of a magical endeavor more holistically, you will see that every phase has a place and purpose. We can use the seasons and the moon to illustrate this. The raising of energy corresponds to spring leading up to the summer solstice or the waxing moon leading up to the full moon. Yet, springtime and the waxing moon are one small part of an entire cycle. In addition, similar to the moon in its full or dark phase, there will be intense moments of culmination and rest throughout your magical process. In cyclical magic, rather than suggesting you cast a circle during the first phase and close your circle in the last phase, I invite you to reserve practices like this for the most intense moments of your magic-making process. If you cast a protective circle in the initial phase of openness and inspiration, you might inadvertently cut yourself off from spirits or allies that desire to work with you. There are degrees of protection, and each phase of your magical cycle will require different techniques and levels of care. Here's a diagram illustrating what this could look like for you:

## Cyclical Magic

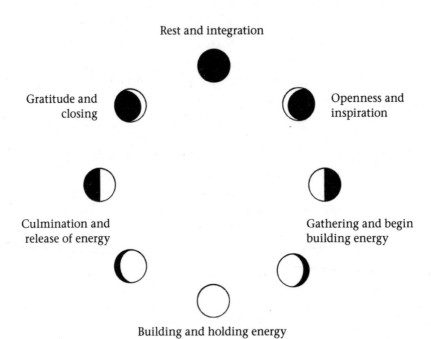

Rest and integration

Gratitude and closing

Openness and inspiration

Culmination and release of energy

Gathering and begin building energy

Building and holding energy

1. Openness and inspiration: Opening yourself to new magical endeavors, spirit guides, and allies.
2. Gathering and begin building energy: Determining your next magical act, connecting with the guides and allies you are being called to work with, and gathering materials and information.
3. Building and holding energy: Deepening your connection with guides and allies, building energy, and final planning and preparations.
4. Culmination and release of energy: Create sacred space, perform your spell or magical action, and begin releasing energy.
5. Gratitude and closing: Continue the release of energy, thank and give offerings to guides and allies.
6. Rest and integration: Tend to yourself, rest, and integrate.

The cycle and illustration is one option. Just like the seasons and phases of the moon, you can view them from the macro—e.g., light half of the year versus dark half of the year or waxing versus waning. You could also go into the micro of each phase by breaking each one into more refined steps. For me, it depends on the kind of magic I'm working and how I'm instructed to work it. Similarly, working cyclically in your magic doesn't mean that every act of magic will be a long endeavor. You might move through all of these cycles in an afternoon—for example, with a short spell—while some magic, like a long-lasting ritual, may span years. What's become important in my practice is ensuring that I am aware of the cycle of each spell and how I may or may not be invited to engage with each phase. For example, if you're crafting magic involving working with energies you're less familiar with, you will likely spend more time in the inspiration and gathering phases, whereas if you're crafting magic with energies you know well, you might breeze through some of the earlier steps and spend more time building and holding energy with them. Furthermore, you don't need to practice these steps consecutively. You might have breaks of days or even weeks between different phases due to the demands of your mundane life or the magical process.

Let's explore ways each phase of crafting magic might show up and possible activities for each phase. As you explore these, I invite you to keep in mind how they might shift and change for different kinds of magic and spellwork. For example, if you're crafting a less complicated spell, what parts might you spend less time with? At first glance, the following might seem completely overwhelming or unattainable. You probably won't do every single thing I offer in this section and I don't expect you to. If working in this way feels overwhelming to you, I invite you to focus on the parts that do feel nourishing and doable. Start there. I also want to point out that even though I'm comparing each phase of the magic-making process with a season or a moon phase, it doesn't mean that they need to align with said season or moon phase. Sometimes they might and sometimes it won't be feasible. We'll discuss this more in the section on sacred timing. As always, all of these offerings are examples from my personal practice and are not intended to be reproduced exactly as I've written here. Take what you like and leave the rest!

### *Openness and inspiration:*

The initial phase of embarking on a magical endeavor aligns with the new moon. It is a time to open yourself to a wide expanse of magical possibility and energetic support from your guides and magical allies. We already discussed much of this phase in the first section of this chapter on human exceptionalism and seeking humility. This phase is often more passive because it focuses on being open to receiving guidance rather than taking direct action on a specific magical desire. However, it is not entirely passive. There is a level of awareness required to know when you are in this phase, and it has a distinct feel that is very different from the integration and rest phase. Rather than resting and integrating, you might feel called to meditate or go for walks, with the intent to be open to guidance from the land or your guides on how to engage with your magic next. If you know where your magic is needed, it might look like opening up to guides and allies for suggestions. In my practice, this phase often looks like going on exploratory journeys where I allow my guides to lead me instead of me deciding where or with whom I want to journey.

This phase also requires discernment. Even though this phase is more passive, risk is involved anytime you intentionally open yourself to new energies, spirits, or sacred spaces. You may find it beneficial to spend time sitting with new inspiration for magic by thoroughly exploring it before determining where to focus your energy. You might liken this phase to the dating or "getting to know you" phase of crafting your magic. I experience this phase as a time to become acutely aware of where my focus is being pulled, noticing who or what is trying to get my attention and running it through my various forms of discernment.

Limiting outside distractions such as social media, as you are able, can be helpful during this phase. It is a time to keep your energy clear, open, and receptive to sifting through the sometimes softer and quieter energies surrounding you. Another part of this phase is knowing when it's time for you to step into it. Sometimes you might want to move into this phase, but the demands of your mundane life don't support it. Frustrating as this can be, my guides usually offer to stay in the rest and integration phase from previous magical workings for a bit longer. It might also be that the energies that want to work with you next are not quite ready or that the timing isn't right.

Possible activities for this phase include the following:

- Walks in nature
- Meditation
- Journeying without a specific goal
- Gentle breathwork
- Freewriting
- Connecting with divinatory tools, such as the tarot
- Being aware of what's catching your attention
- Considering where your magic might be most needed in your life, family, or the collective
- Opening up to guides and magical allies for guidance
- Doing any other activities that help you be in a state of awareness and receptivity

### Gathering and begin building energy:

This phase corresponds with the waxing moon and springtime. It signals a time of committing to a new magical project through gathering and building energy. Gathering in this phase can pertain to gathering information, correspondences, allies, or materials. You may sense that a strong theme of openness and awareness remains for this phase as you become attuned to the magical project. The most significant shift in this phase is that you may sense building energy and feel called to begin taking action. Sometimes the energy building is intentional, while other times it happens organically, especially when other energy cycles, like the phase of the moon, seasons, or astrological events align with your magic. For example, this phase can feel especially intense if you're in this phase when the moon is waxing.

To intentionally build energy in this phase, you might connect more deeply with those you feel called to work with. Let's use the example of collaborating with the element of water. If you are working with the element of water for your magic, you might journey to the spirit of water, connect with water physically in a mindful state, and create art to channel or connect with the spirit of water. All these will help deepen your relationship with water and the magic you are making together. You can also begin widening your community of correspondences for your magic to invite in new energies and consider the best timing for your magic. (We will discuss timing in the next section.) For example, revisiting working with water, you might journal or freewrite about other energies that resonate with the element of water. Doing so can shed light on different energies that correspond with the element of water and the essence of the magic you're crafting. All of these steps can build and intensify the energy for your magical work.

This phase can require more trust than the others, especially when you feel pulled to work with energies that are new to you or in ways that are new and different. It's usually in this phase when I sometimes notice a feeling of *Oh, crap. What did I sign up for?* If this happens, I encourage you to give yourself extra space to be in the process rather than focus on moving ahead. You may find some nuggets of wisdom or insight hidden inside your fears. This is one reason why, over the years, I've increasingly favored slow magic. Slow magic happens over a more extended period, maybe several months or even years. So much of our human world runs on a false sense of urgency; your magical practice isn't immune to this. I've been shown repeatedly, usually in this phase, that slowing down will serve me and the magical project, especially if I'm feeling nervous or hurried. Remember, time is a human construct, and many of our more-than-human allies and spirit guides do not run on the same schedule!

If your magical work requires physical materials, you might begin feeling called to gather them in this phase. This can inspire a sense of building momentum and is another beautiful opportunity to deepen your relationship with those you're working with. Knowing where to gather is an opportunity to lean on your intuitive abilities. As you gather materials, you'll have opportunities to connect physically and ask for consent and guidance for your magic. As the energy for your magic continues to grow and move closer to the next phase, you may want to connect more regularly with those you're working with for continued guidance and support and to deepen your relationship. The continued connection with the different energies I'm working with is essential in my practice, as it helps sync our intentions and energy with action. This phase is also a great time to begin writing down any steps or processes for your magic, including when and how you intend to enact your magic.

Possible activities for this phase include the following:

- Connect with specific energies involved in the magic via physical contact, meditation, journeying, or another way you prefer.

- Explore your personal circle of correspondences to better understand and connect with the energies present for the magic, invite new energies into your community, and begin planning timing.

- Allow space in your practice, as you are able, for activities that help you feel grounded and supported so you can remain tuned in to those you're working with. This might include maintaining a breathwork, meditation, or somatic practice.

- Gather or make materials needed for the magic— ritually and mindfully.

- Write or journal ideas, steps, or invocations for the magic.

- Request consent from the energies involved in the magic.

## *Building and holding energy:*

Comparing this phase to the wheel of seasons, it corresponds with summertime. This phase can be more physically demanding and active, and you might sense a lot going on. If you do, building in additional time for practices that help you feel grounded and supported can be helpful. Like a wave beginning to crest, you may find that the energy of your magic continues to intensify organically. You've laid the groundwork to expand into this phase; now it's time to ride the wave. By this phase, you will likely be well connected to all of the energies, spirits, and allies you are working with for your magic. Because of this, you might find that guidance and support for your magic flows in with ease. You might be intuitively guided to practice techniques that help build energy, like intense somatic practices, chanting, breathwork, channeling, or trance states. If these things aren't happening or you're not sure how to move forward, honor it as an invitation to reconnect to those you're working with.

Channeling or moving in and out of trance states might happen unprompted in this phase. If this is new for you, it can be jarring. It might feel like you're merging your subtle body, or personal energy field, with those you're working with, or like you're entering into a temporary portal of otherworldly space. If you feel this happening and you're up to exploring it, go for it. It has the potential to deeply inform your magic. Alternatively, if this feels scary or uncomfortable, don't engage and ask for it to stop. Working with a mentor can be valuable in situations when you're navigating new intuitive and magical terrain.

It is within this phase that holding or being with the buildup of energy takes place. For some magical workings, this might be a few minutes, or it could be several days. If working in this way is new to you, begin with shorter lengths of time (30–60 minutes) and work up to larger stretches of time (one to several days). What this feels like for each person will vary. For me, the buildup and holding of energy often feels like an electrical current pulsing through my body. I usually have more energy. My body sometimes feels like it's literally buzzing, and I become incredibly sensitive to other energies and physical stimulation. To continue to build and hold this energy, you might find it important to take special care of your physical needs by eating nourishing meals and moving your body as you're able. You might also notice that you experience sleep disturbances. If you do, remember they won't be permanent. Due to how sensitive this phase can make you feel, leaning on your energy protection and maintenance practice can be supportive. We all have different constitutions. Listen to your body and honor it as best you can in this phase.

As you sense energy building within and around you, you may notice it's time to make final refinements in your planning and timing. It's almost time to engage in any remaining actions to release your magic. As you near the tipping point of your magic, keep in mind that you are working collaboratively. Being guided to make last-minute changes is not uncommon. I've learned the hard way not to plan or time things out too early in this process as I'm sometimes guided to shift course. There have been several mornings when I woke up and did not have anything planned, yet I suddenly knew it was time to move into the culmination phase of a magical working. This might present as an inner knowing, auditory download, or visual in your mind that indicates to you that it's time to move to the next phase. Over time, if you don't already, you will learn what this feels like in your body too.

During this phase, consider the following activities:

- Grounding practices like dancing, eating nourishing foods for your body, and spending time outside

- Engaging in trance or channeling to further your connection with those you're working with

- Ensuring all needed materials for your magic are ready

- Refining your magical plans as any new guidance comes in

- Engaging in "mundane" self-care practices like a hot bath or self-massage
- Engaging in energetic protection practices like setting boundaries, working with protective stones, or calling in guides or allies you work with for protection

### *Culmination and release of energy:*

 This phase aligns with the time between the summer solstice and autumn. In late summer, flowers are in full bloom and plants are ripening. Like the earth in this phase, it's time to let your magic be on full display and come to fruition! When you're engaged in particularly intense or long magical endeavors, this phase can feel like a long-awaited performance. Nervous energy is normal and something you can use to fuel your magic. This is the phase that most magical books focus on, but as you can see, there's so much that can happen behind the scenes before and after this phase. Without the other phases, it can feel like going through the motions instead of being deeply embedded and supported by a wider network of magical and more-than-human allies. With culmination also comes a time of surrender and release. You've opened yourself up and listened, collaborated with your magical and spiritual community of guides and allies, built and held energy by continuing to deepen your connection with those you're working with, and gathered materials and prepared yourself. Now it is time to release the magic you've co-created out into the world.

Once you commit to this part of the process, it's time to gather any materials you intend to work alongside, get to where you intend to enact your magic, and start preparing yourself and the space. With how much energy you've already poured into this, you may sense the true weight and sacredness of working collaboratively and communally in your magic. If you do, it's something to be treasured. To honor the sacredness of this moment, you might feel called to energetically cleanse yourself, any materials, and your space. Use a technique aligned with your practice; it could include cleansing with smoke, salt, or water. Once you've done this, you can cast a circle or create a sacred space in a way that aligns with your practice. There are many ways to do this and it varies culturally. You might call upon the four elements, work with a staff or wand to draw a circle around you and your space, work with crystals or minerals, such as salt, to create a circle, or ask your guides to support you with this. If unsure, pause and tune in to those you are collaborating with for this magical endeavor.

Firmly in your sacred space, the physical acts of crafting your magic can now transpire. It is at this time that your physical human body brings something unique to the magic. You may be able to move your body and perform physical acts that those you're working with cannot (in a collaborative way rather than a dominating way), and that is something to be celebrated. For example, if you're working closely with a tree spirit, the tree spirit may be thrilled to cocreate with a human who has the ability to carve a magical item from its bark. The physical crafting of your magic can take many different forms, some of which I'll outline later in this chapter. This could be dressing and lighting a candle, preparing a spell jar, crafting a flower essence, or something new and unusual. I want to really stress this last bit, as it is truly the core of this book! Please allow your magic be as creative as you are invited to make it.

To know when the energy of this magical working has reached its fullest expression and is ready to be released will be an intuitive decision. It will be helpful to stay engaged with those you've been working with throughout this process, to know when this time comes. As the physical magic unfolds, it is possible to again experience moments of trance or channeling as you continue to engage with and possibly enmesh yourself with those you're working alongside. There might be a physical action, such as the moment a candle flame goes out, the end of a chant, or maybe just an internal knowing that it's time to release all of the energy you've been building and holding. If you are working on a longer or more intense spell, this moment of release can feel intense, and you might need to initially sit or lie down. Try to honor your body and the intuitive information you receive.

You might feel called to end this phase with a phrase like "so it is," "so mote it be," or even a simple "thank you." This too can be intuitive. Once you feel complete in this phase, you can release your circle and any energy you may have called upon to create your sacred space. I will invite you to engage in gratitude and giving offerings in a later phase, but you might feel called to connect with and thank each of the guides and allies you have worked with. It can also be supportive to have some food and drink to help ground yourself into your body and the physical environment. Similar to the building of energy, the releasing of energy will not be an instantaneous event. Releasing the energy of this magical endeavor will continue on after this phase. This phase is the initiatory spark that both begins—and culminates—the releasing process of your magic.

Possible activities for this phase include the following:

- Prepare yourself and your space for the culmination of the magical project.

- Cast a circle, call quarters, or use any other form of creating a sacred and supportive space to conduct the magic.

- Call in any magical allies or guides you've collaborated with who wish to be present during your magical project.

- Allow the energy of your magic to intensify if it feels applicable to the magic. You could do this by dancing or intuitively moving your body, chanting, singing, playing an instrument, or any other way you feel called to assist in the culmination of the magic.

- Perform whatever magic spell or ritual you wish, and initiate the release of energy.

- Close your circle or sacred space with special words of closing or thanks.

- Tend to your physical body after conducting the magic by consuming nourishing food and drink.

## *Gratitude and closing:*

In the waning moon or autumn phase of your magic, you have the opportunity to give thanks and offerings to all who made the magic possible. It is also a time to continue to release the buildup of energy you were enmeshed in throughout the previous phases. In this phase you will begin consciously disengaging from the energy currents you collectively built with those you were working with. This might look like tending more to your mundane needs and practicing more passive and relaxing energy maintenance such as taking gentle walks, observing the breath rather than practicing more active breathwork, or doing a body scan visualization rather than a more active somatic practice.

Before you close this magical cycle, it can be helpful to tune in to those you were working with one more time to ensure there aren't any final actions or considerations for you to assist with. If you've been working with a specific crystal for this magical cycle, you could do this by holding it in your hands and asking if there's anything you missed or should tend to before you begin a closing ritual and give offerings. Remember, this can all happen over several days and need not all happen at once.

You may have offered initial words of gratitude and thanks in the previous phase, but often more is desired and necessary. This can be such a supportive and nurturing part of your cycle of magic for you and the guides and allies you worked with. You might find it supportive to create a closing ritual at this part in the process. Closing rituals can look like a lot of things and can vary in complexity. Common closing rituals might include giving offerings to those you worked with, returning organic materials to the earth, taking a cleansing bath, or lighting a candle. If the magic you created resulted in a final product, such as an herbal creation, the finished product can make a wonderful offering. I create flower essences often and like to offer some of the finished essence to any of the plant spirits that assisted in the process. For smaller magical workings, a closing ritual might be as simple as closing your eyes and taking a few conscious breaths while thanking yourself and the spirits that guided you.

This phase of the magic is also a time to wrap up any loose ends and perform any final mundane tasks required for your magic, such as bottling up any herbal creations, cleaning (physically or energetically) magical materials, and tidying up your magical space. Though this might seem more mundane, the energetic effects of these actions can be very supportive in the closing phase. As you engage in these more mundane needs, you may sense the intensity of previous phases slowly dissipating from your body. Each closing ritual and action helps facilitate this.

Possible activities for this phase include the following:

- Giving offerings
- Cleansing and clearing
- Returning organic materials to the earth
- Performing closing rituals
- Conducting final steps required to fulfill the magic
- Slowing down and disengaging from the intuitive energies you've been working with

### Rest and integration:

In a world where the dominant culture praises action and perpetual doing, I cannot overstate the importance of this phase enough! You deserve rest. We all do. Allowing yourself ample time to integrate your magical cycle may initially feel uncomfortable. I encourage you to notice how soon after engaging in a magical cycle you feel like starting another one. Before you engage in any new magic, pause, check in with your body, and ask yourself if you've had enough time to integrate truly. I still catch myself trying to rush to the next spell or magical working. FOMO can certainly extend into your magical practice!

This phase might look like stepping away from crafting any magic. This is okay; in fact, it's great! Pauses like this allow you to properly assimilate everything that transpired in the previous cycle to create rich compost for a new cycle of magic. This doesn't mean you can't practice any of your energy or spiritual maintenance. During this phase, it can be supportive to ground into your most beloved daily ritual practices, such as lighting incense, pulling a tarot or oracle card for the day, connecting with your altar space, or a doing a simple breathing or meditation practice.

When you ignore the death phase in your magical practice, it forces you to stay the same. By embracing death phases, you open yourself up to transforming in new and needed ways. Fully honoring this phase does more than help to close the magical workings and restore yourself fully; it also prepares you for future magical workings. Like mundane work, if you hop from project to project with no time for rest or reflection, your work will undoubtedly suffer. The magical world is similar in this way. You will likely notice new layers of insight and wisdom as you allow yourself time to pause your magical practice. The cycles and timelines of other beings are often quite different than our human perception of time. There will be no shortage of magical endeavors to explore when you know it's time to start back up. My spirit guides and allies are rather loud when it's time for me to come back to my practice. I have no doubt they will be for you too.

Possible activities for this phase include the following:

- Resting as you are able

- Doing reflective journaling

- Doing restorative practices such as body scans, and meditations or walks with the intent to observe rather than connect

- Returning fully to the mundane aspects of your life

- Savoring all that the mundane world has to offer

- Rooting into your most beloved daily rituals
- Resisting the urge to start another magical project too soon

## Cyclical Magic Example

Here's an example of how I apply each of these steps to a shorter magical project that spans four days. In my practice, I collaborate with tree and plant spirits often by crafting essences. Essences, also called flower essences, is a form of working with the energetics of plants, trees, and even fungi collaboratively with water. For this particular example, the days are not consecutive. This is often the case for me, either due to the demands of my mundane life or the natural progression of the magic.

### *Day One*

**Openness and inspiration phase:** As I connect with the plants around my house, I notice that the hawthorn tree in my yard will be flowering soon. I work with this tree often and have an established relationship with it. I ask it if it would like me to work with it in its flowering phase in any specific way. An essence feels like a "yes," and I gratefully agree to work with it in this way.

**Gathering and building energy phase:** I spend my morning journeying to connect with the hawthorn tree energetically in the spirit realm. I am able to understand and connect with the energy of its flowering phase when I do. As a result I better understand the purpose and uses of the essence we will create. I begin preparing and collecting the items needed to create the essence.

### *Day Two*

**Building and holding energy phase:** I continue to connect with the hawthorn tree physically and energetically as I continue to gather materials. My understanding of its energy and the purpose of the magic deepens, and I continue to feel the energy building. I begin becoming aware of timing. I check the timing of the moon phase and zodiac signs and realize that a full moon in Sagittarius will likely align perfectly with the blossoming flowers. I check this with my guides and the hawthorn tree and receive a "yes" to continue with this plan.

## Day Three

**Action and release of energy phase:** The full moon arrives and, after connecting with the hawthorn tree again, I determine that creating the essence on the waxing side of the full moon in Sagittarius is ideal. I ensure I have time blocked off to tend to the physical actions required to make the essence. When the time is right, I collect the materials needed and bring them outside around the tree. I cleanse myself and all of my materials with incense. I take time to connect with the earth, my breath, and my body. I cast a circle and allow the energy that's been building to culminate. I begin crafting the essence by carefully engaging with the hawthorn tree and asking it which flowers it would like me to cut for the essence. While doing so, a nearby rosebush catches my attention. I connect with rose and hawthorn and confirm that a rose should be added to the essence. I am in a trancelike state for the duration of this process. I continue to hold the space as the flowers sit in the water and create the essence. When the essence is complete, I thank the hawthorn tree and the rosebush, bottle the mother essence, and close the space by releasing the circle. I offer words of thanks to the hawthorn tree and the rosebush before cleaning up my materials. I place the bottled mother essence in a prepared sacred space until I am able to dilute it into stock bottles.

## Day Four

**Gratitude and closing phase:** When time allows and all feels aligned, I prepare my items for the final phase of diluting the mother essence into stock bottles. I again cleanse the items and myself and call upon the elements to guide and protect as I work. Once the stock bottles are prepared, I go to the hawthorn tree and rosebush and offer them several drops of the finished essence. I thank them again for their guidance and participation.

**Rest and integration phase:** I take a break from crafting any new magic for a few days. I tend to my mundane life. I think about and process the magic that took place with Hawthorn and Rose. I am subtly aware of incoming information about how the energetic magic created in the essence wants to be utilized. I do not take action but know that this information will be there when I need it.

As you explore crafting cyclical magic, you will find a rhythm that works for you and become more familiar with how each phase feels. One of the beautiful parts of working more cyclically is that you'll eventually be able to intuitively recognize when it's time to move into a new phase. Your rhythms and cycles will look different throughout various phases of your life and will certainly look different from mine; this is to be expected. Let's explore how timing can support you in your magical processes.

### Intentional Timing

If you honor the moon, stars, and seasons, you probably already know that some seasons and times hold unique energy. These various energies can be woven throughout your magic to inform and support it. Perhaps you already feel drawn to certain astrological, lunar, or earthly seasons. If you do, this is a sign you're already tuned in to their energetic influences. I am often drawn to eclipse seasons for magical endeavors. Now that I know this, I'm better prepared for these seasons. For you, it may be full moons, springtime, or during planetary retrograde seasons. In this section, we'll examine the difference between working with energetic beings versus the energetics of timing, and different kinds of energy fluctuations, including how they can weave through your magic.

Let's explore similarities and differences between your relationships with a spirit or singular energy and a cycle of time—e.g., a crystal compared to the moon's phases. Because I rely heavily on clairsentience (clear feeling), I'll explain how I experience these two kinds of energy and offer some ways they could appear for you. For me, the energy of a crystal or a plant feels more contained, while the energy of a new moon feels like a subtle energy that blankets and touches everything. If you are primarily clairvoyant (clear seeing), you might experience varying intensities of visualizations during full moons versus the dark moon, whereas how you visualize the energy of a tree might remain consistent. In the same way these energy phases affect you, they also affect the animate world around you. This is especially visible in the plant world, where plants react to both the cycles of the seasons and the moon. These subtle energy fluctuations that touch everything are what we are discussing here.

To make intentional timing even more interesting, various energy fluctuations can occur at a given moment. You will experience them to different degrees and in different ways. Some people are more sensitive to the moon's phases, while others may be more sensitive to the movement of the stars. The phases of the moon, seasons of the earth, zodiac seasons, planetary motions, numerological influences, eclipse seasons, time of day, day of the week, and even celebrations and holidays can add various layers of energy to your magic. On a personal level, you also experience cycles with your age, seasons of life—maiden, mother, or crone, etc.— and menstruation. I've undoubtedly left some out because so many of these influences are cultural. This will be another area that is varied and unique for each practitioner. As usual, what's most important is your relationship with the different cycles of timing you value most and how you choose, or are called, to weave them into your magic. I will primarily reference the phases of the moon, seasons of the earth, and zodiac seasons here, as they are the primary cycles of timing that I work with. However, you can apply most of what I offer here to any cycle of time or event.

Most cycles of time contain phases of increasing energy and decreasing energy, as well as more concentrated points of death and rebirth. Some events seem more isolated, such as a total solar eclipse or moving into your crone phase. Although these seem like isolated events, if you zoom out, you might find that even these are part of larger cycles. Understanding these currents on a personal and collective level and how to work with them can help you understand your energy and the rhythms within your magical practice. As I mentioned, you will likely notice specific energetic events that you feel more pulled to work with. When you do, and one of these times rolls around, it can be an excellent time to consider stepping into the first phase of your magical cycle by opening yourself to possible magical projects.

One of my favorite ways to work with timing is to be aware of times when two or more cycles of time sync their energy; I call these "magical windows." For example, if you know new moons light you up and a new moon is approaching on the spring equinox at the start of Aries season, buckle up! That's a solid invitation to work some potent magic. Other examples include the following:

- A full moon at the summer solstice

- A dark moon during menstruation

- A waxing moon in the sign of Sagittarius on a Thursday

Not all of these may resonate with you, but you'll find your windows of magic that do. When you know what energies are being amplified at a given moment and that the animate world around you likely feels it too, it can help to inform and guide your magic.

You can reference all sorts of information about what each season, moon phase, day of week, etc., represents and the energy it carries. I will always encourage you to personally connect with these cycles of time first so you can form a deeper connection with them from your unique lens. You likely already have a sense of the overarching energies of many of them because you've lived with them all your life! Here are some activities and questions to help you explore different cycles of time and how they might affect you and your practice:

- How do you feel during a new moon, waxing moon, full moon, waning moon, or dark moon? Consider allowing yourself time to meditate or reflect on each moon phase as it comes and goes.

- Are there phases of the moon that seem to make it easier or harder to connect with different energies you work with, like plants, stones, or the elements?

- Are there certain energies that you gravitate toward during specific moon phases or seasons? Consider exploring those relationships and what insights they might have for you.

- How do you feel as the seasons shift, and how does the environment around you feel in each new season? Consider allowing yourself time to meditate or reflect on each season as it comes and goes.

- Do you notice changes in your energy levels in different phases of the moon, seasons, or weekdays?

- When cycles of time sync up and there's an amplification of a specific kind of energy, how do you feel and what kind of effect does it have on your magical practice?

- Are their specific zodiac seasons you feel more or less resonant with? What about them feels more or less resonant?

- Are there specific cycles of time that were important to your ancestors? If so, how connected to them do you feel?

- If you've identified specific phases of cycles when you tend not to feel well, have you found any energies to help balance or soothe your feelings?

Sometimes life happens, and even with your best intentions, timing might not go as you hope. So, what do you do when you miss your window of magic or you feel like you should craft some magic but don't have the physical or mental capacity? There will likely be times when you have plans to perform a phase of your magic during a perfectly timed magical window, and then your kid sprains their ankle, you get called in to work, or your partner gets sick, and your window is gone. When this happens, start by connecting with the circle of energies you're working with for the magical endeavor (psst, they'll probably already know!). When you do, they're able to offer insight and guide you in your next steps. Sometimes you might later realize that these interruptions were intentional. The beauty of understanding corresponding energies is that there are ways to help compensate mismatched energy caused by timing. For example, if you hoped to conclude a magical project on the dark moon but missed the window and the moon has shifted into a new moon phase, you could look to your circle of correspondences to determine other times or energies that align with the dark moon that could help to soften the new moon energy present.

The energy present from cycles of time and events can be an important part of your practice, but they don't need to dictate everything you do. Make space for nuance and lean on your relationships with your guides and magical allies when you're unsure. There might be times when you feel pulled to craft magic during cycles when other practitioners firmly advise against it, such as during eclipse and retrograde seasons. Trust where you're guided with your discernment in hand, and know that you can always change your mind.

## Magical Approaches

Crafting magic solely on your magical and spiritual relationships, ethical framework, and intuition *is enough* and your magic does not need to look like anyone else's to be meaningful, real, and powerful. Working in this way requires deep trust. Yet, it can also be helpful to know some of the common modes available for crafting magic, especially if you are new to this world. That said, I will not be sharing specific spells or rituals to utilize them; that would be something for you to explore. Remember, this is a book that helps you to *craft your own magic*. Your magical relationships, intuitive abilities, and ethical framework provide a deep well of meaningful magic. However, seeking out specific guidance around crafting magic, especially those connected to your lineage, can be deeply nourishing and helpful. You can wisely and intentionally merge the call to craft your own magic with other sources. My desire is to bring some balance to it.

## Common Ways to Craft Magic

Think far beyond what I offer here and allow your creativity and relationships with your guides to build upon these offerings. If you do desire more information on any of the modes of magic-making offered here, you can find several books in the bibliography that have influenced my practice, or seek out guidance unique to your ancestry. Finally, keep in mind that it is also okay if your magic does not look anything like what I share here, or if it is a combination of various techniques.

**Candles** – Candles are a personal favorite mode of crafting magic and they are used ubiquitously worldwide. Candles represent all four elements: the melting wax represents water; the wick—earth; the flame—fire; and the smoke—air. With the four elements present, candles offer a potent means of shifting energy. Candles are also a wonderful way to incorporate other energies that may desire to work collaboratively with you. You can carve symbols on the outside of the candle, roll the candle in herbs, or place crystals in or around the candle to narrow the focus of your magical workings.

**Spell bottles and jars** – Another common mode of crafting magic cross-culturally is through bottles and jars. Magic like this can be worked with any kind of container, though the container you choose can certainly affect the magic. The receptacle you choose serves as a container for your magical workings and can vary vastly in size, complexity, and purpose. All elements, including any other ingredients meaningful to the magic, can easily be combined into a jar. Spell jars and bottles are ideal for working with fluids and are more permanent in nature because they can be preserved or buried, though they do not need to be.

**Magic, charm, and spell bags** – Similar in some ways to working with jars and bottles, charm and spell bags can contain a multitude of items and energies and be utilized for several different purposes. They differ from spell jars in their portability, and they can appear innocuous, making them ideal for magic you might like to wear or utilize in more public settings. Similar to jars and bottles, the bag itself—its color, material, how it's made, and anything you might stitch or draw to the bag itself—can add a lot of depth to your magical workings. These also have more culturally specific names, such as mojo bags.

**Water and essences** – As we explored in Chapter 4 on the topic of correspondences, water is an excellent communicator and connector. Crafting essences falls within the realm of water magic, but is a separate craft in and of itself that can vary in complexity. The way to work with water can be as vast as the many ways that water can present itself. Water can hold energy, making it an ideal way to share information and energy. Some of my favorite ways of working with water include crafting essences, giving offerings, channeling and trance work, doing cleansing rituals, and taking magical baths.

**Energy healing and journeying** – Many magic practitioners rely solely on their ability to engage with energy. Hands-on and remote healing is common in many cultural practices. Working in this way can extend far beyond the human realm and include plants, animals, land, and more. Energy work also includes those who journey or practice astral projection as a means of tending to energetic realms and beings. This can include ancestral healing, offering healing to other parts of the world and time-lines, communicating with other beings, and serving as a psychopomp. Many of these techniques require training and initiation. If you feel yourself pulled to this kind of work, I encourage you to explore it.

**Smoke and fire** – This is another common magical companion worldwide. Smoke is often worked with as a means of healing, giving offerings, clearing, and serving a role in protective magical workings. It commonly includes the use of intentionally selected herbs and plant materials. Fire is a common magical partner in transformation and releasing magic, though not always. Smoke and fire can also be used as a form of divination. These two elements, especially in combination with certain plants, have also been affected by commodification, extraction, and cultural appropriation. I encourage you to be mindful when including the use of herbs and trees with your smoke and fire magic to ensure you're not participating in closed practices that might require specific training and permission.

**Words, symbols, and sigils** – Words—both spoken and written—as well as various symbols and sigils are wonderful tools for crafting magic that practitioners have been working with since time immemorial. The simplicity or complexity of working with magic in these ways are just as varied. Chanting, mantras, poetry, and song all have the potential to be worked with magically and often are, whether knowingly or not. These methods can be beautiful ways to give offerings or shift the energy of space. Sigils are a unique form of magic-making I'm particularly fond of that fall into this category. Sigils are a written form of spellwork that involves creating a unique symbol from the text; the resulting symbol is imbued with a specific intention. Sigils are highly portable and can hold a great deal of energy and information.

**Stones and crystals** – Magic practitioners worldwide use stones and crystals, and their use varies vastly from culture to culture. Working with crystals and stones is an area of magic that has been more prominently affected by human commodification and extraction. If you want to work with stones or crystals, I encourage you to do so with a heavy reliance on your magical ethical framework and discernment. Similar to water, many crystals can hold information and energy, but in contrast, they can also serve as antennae of sorts, making it easier to direct energy. Stones and crystals can be ideal for adding or amplifying specific energy in your magical workings, like jars, bags, and candle spells. Stones are often used for various forms of healing magic.

**Rope and cord** – Though this is, in my opinion, a less frequently discussed mode of crafting magic, it is one I'd love to see make a comeback. Rope and cord magic was and is common among many of my ancestors and is often worked with as a way to tie up, bind, or hold specific energy. Material, timing, and the number of strands or knots can all hold significance when working magic in this way. I enjoy working with rope and cord because I find that its uses are unique, accessible, and easily transportable.

**Plants and trees** – There are rich and diverse magical practices all over the world that involve herbs, flowers, plants, and trees. Many folk magic practices rely heavily on the plant world, and for good reason. Much of our food and medicine have been and continue to be contingent upon our relationships with the plant world. This is yet another area of crafting magic that requires deep reliance on discernment and a magical ethical framework. Many trees and plants are extinct or endangered due to human action and inaction. Though plants are often used in combination with other magical methods, they are powerful in their own right. Simply tending to plants by listening to their needs is an act of magic.

**Movement and dance** – Your body is a powerhouse of magic that holds all the elements and can be worked with individually or in groups to create magic. We can see individual examples of this in various breathwork and somatic practices, and group examples reflected in the act of raising energy, often done by moving or dancing around a fire or inducing trance through dance. Some forms of working magic with the body might include utilizing tools such as rattles or feathers, but not always. Working with your body can also be a great source of alchemizing energy to assist with energy clearing or healing for yourself or others. It is also an ideal way to give offerings or to personalize your magical workings with various bodily fluids.

This is a small sampling of ways to craft magic in your practice. As your practice deepens, you will find your preferred methods of crafting magic. Similar to your closest magical allies, your preferred (or chosen) forms of magic will surface over time. Allowing this to happen will enable you to form your personal preferences and methods unique to you and your craft. You might even stumble upon or be invited into modes of crafting magic completely unknown to you. Though practicing in ways you've never heard of can feel scary initially, the creative process is a needed and necessary part of crafting your own magic. We need inventors in the magical world too, and you might find that your unique form of magic is something quite needed.

## Altars and Sacred Spaces

Similar to timing, location in your magic can also make an impact. Altars are used by all kinds of magical practitioners, past and present, to cultivate, contain, or work

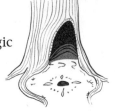

with different energy. For this reason, they can serve as a powerful ally in conducting magic. Let's differentiate between altars and sacred spaces. Altars are human-made areas or structures intended to honor a specific purpose or beings. While an altar can also be a sacred space, a sacred space is not always an altar. Sacred spaces can present in different areas due to unique features in the land—like a specific group of trees, a body of water, a mountain—or due to energy that was cultivated in an area from other people. An example of the latter could include a sacred spring or rock formation used in antiquity for magical purposes. Let's explore some of the ways you can collaborate with altars and sacred spaces.

Altars are common in magical, spiritual, and religious practices. Some altars require exact construction while others are informal. In my opinion, the nature of how an altar might be constructed bears little weight on the depth of meaning and magical power it holds. Altars also have vast uses and purposes. Allow your relationship with creating and using an altar to be personal and creative. It certainly isn't required or necessary to work with an altar to have a meaningful magical practice, but you might find that working with one is not only supportive but practical. There are two common purposes for working with altars in a magical practice that I'll focus on here. The first is having a sacred space to store important items in your craft and a space to craft your magic. The second is that it provides a physical location to honor, connect with, and give offerings to the various spirits, allies, deities, and energies you work with. These two purposes could be used on either the same or separate altars. Or you might become altar-obsessed, like me, and find that you want to create altars of all shapes and sizes all around your home and on favorite outside spots. I wouldn't fault you if you did. Altars are magical.

I've noticed in working one-on-one with folks that there's sometimes trepidation or fear when it comes to making an altar. Though I do believe a healthy level of respect for your altar is important, I don't subscribe to many of the rules some associate with creating and using an altar. Much of this trepidation comes from rules about altars that have come from Wicca or other religions. In many folk magic practices, and in the case of crafting your own magic, altars can be personal and will likely be heavily influenced by both your local environment and your ancestry. I encourage you to be playful and creative with a healthy dose of respect when it comes to creating altars. Revisit the ancestor altar exercise in Chapter 2 for the basic steps to create an altar.

By creating altars, you are creating a sacred space, but sacred spaces don't require human touch. As you explore your local environment, physically or through spiritual journey, you will likely come across sacred spaces in the natural world or in seemingly random modern places. Noticing and interacting with these kinds of sacred spaces can become an important and influential part of your practice. You might find that you're drawn to specific locations for specific magical workings. Engaging with sacred spaces that aren't your altars comes with an entirely different approach. I encourage you to engage with sacred spaces outside of your home with a deep level of care and respect because they may not be for you to engage with, especially in a magical capacity. I encourage you to rely on much of what we discussed in the chapter on relationship when approaching sacred spaces outside of your living area, especially when it comes to consent and permission. There are entire forested areas that I do not step foot on because I've received an intuitive "hell no, sister." That said, there are many other sacred spaces that I've found to be welcoming, healing, and important parts of crafting magic.

### Connecting with Sacred Spaces

If you suspect you have found or know of a sacred space with which you want to connect, here is an exercise to try. Connecting with sacred spaces can be an acquired practice requiring honed intuition and a relationship with your environment or the environment in which you intend to connect. You can modify this exercise to connect with a space in your local environment or spiritually journey to a sacred space you know of, such as a sacred well or mountain in your ancestral lands.

1.  Attempt to gain consent. If you have not received an explicit invitation to connect with the sacred space (from a spirit of place at the sacred space, guide, or ancestor), consider tuning in intuitively to gain consent before proceeding. If you cannot gain consent, it is best to wait and continue making contact intuitively until you receive permission. If you happen to stumble upon a sacred space or are visiting one, it doesn't mean you can't view it or even interact with it (although there might be times when you are intuitively asked to leave), but it does mean it is likely in your best interest not to engage any further.

2.  If you receive permission, prepare to connect with the sacred space, including tending your energetic maintenance to ensure you're not bringing any unwanted energies and are intuitively "on" for a visit. This might also include intuitively asking if you could bring any specific offerings. Plan your visit as you are able by carving out time to visit and preparing your offering in advance.

3. When you arrive, move with care, regardless of whether you are connecting in the flesh or through a spiritual journey. Forming these kinds of connections can be energetically, physically, and spiritually exciting and powerful. Moving with the intention of care and respect amidst your excitement can help foster trust. Engaging with your senses while you connect can help you remain embodied if you sense your energy shifting and changing faster than usual.

4. Connect to the sacred space by opening yourself energetically and intuitively as much as you feel safe. During an initial connection, you might be content to simply be present in the space. A simple body scan paired with conscious breathing can be a powerful way to connect in and of itself! You might stop here and skip to step 6 to disengage from the sacred space.

5. If it feels appropriate, consider connecting in other ways through touch (if available) or by intuitively asking questions in the space. What you ask will likely be situational, depending on the nature of the sacred space. A simple starting place can be, "Are there any benevolent beings or spirit of place who would like to share something with me?"

6. Spend as much time connecting as you want or can. When you feel ready to disengage your connection, thank any beings or spirits who came forward and the land or structure itself. Intuitively ask where to leave your offering if you previously asked what you could bring. If you did not do this in advance, ask if you can bring something later or offer something on the spot, like a song or a prayer. If you're encouraged to bring something specific at a later time, be sure to follow up.

7. When you are away from the sacred space and able, spend some time tending to your physical body. You may

be overwhelmed with emotions. Be tender with yourself and consider having some food and drink, gently rocking back and forth, or hugging yourself to help ground.

8. Process and follow up. You might feel called to process your experience through journaling or sharing it with a trusted mentor or magical friend. If your visit requires any follow-up, be it further visits (in my practice, frequent visits are common when I intend to work magic at or with a sacred space), offerings, or to connect again, try to follow up. Remember, if you traveled to a sacred space and cannot return physically, you can always connect in the spirit realm.

Some might also refer to a sacred space as a portal, or an entry to otherworld. Discussing sacred spaces as portals or entries to otherworld could easily be a book in and of itself, so know that this is a very brief explanation. If your interest is piqued, I encourage you to explore myths, stories, and practices from your culture, as many of them reference various kinds of sacred spaces and ways to work with them. In relation to crafting your own magic, sacred spaces can come into play because they sometimes offer unique areas where it can be easier to commune with otherworld energies and information. These spaces can be incredibly helpful when it comes to accessing trance states, journeying, receiving or stepping into intuitive information, crafting magic, connecting with various guides and spirits, and giving offerings. You might find that some spells, rituals, or those you collaborate with want the magic crafted in a specific location. Sacred spaces can be a powerful place to give offerings. You might identify specific sacred spaces where you connect with and give offerings to local land spirits or specific guides. Similar to altars, working with sacred spaces requires curiosity, with a big helping of respect.

# CONCLUSION

As your journey with crafting magic unfolds, remember that the elements and their corresponding wisdom are ever-present. Find them in the sky, land, sea, wind, and your body. Your magical guides and teachers are truly always with you. Picking up and stitching these truths back into your body and soul is the path. Notice when honoring your magic and the magic around you feels impossible due to pervasive themes of linearity, domination, and productivity. It is a privilege to witness, name, and tend to that which has attempted to sever you from your magic. Grieve and rage at the severances you uncover while giving them a soft space to land.

Remember that your magical relationships are fallible and will wax and wane throughout your journey. These relationships are the crux of your magical practice. When your steadfastness wavers, let it, but know that you will be welcomed with deep compassion when you return. The ripples your magical relationships create keep the inner and outer cycles moving. Your trust in them will grow as your roots deepen and expand like those of a Sycamore tree precariously balanced on the edge of a river.

Crafting magic has never been about transcending the body but a deep reverence for the physical and how it intertwines with the unseen realms. When you craft your own magic on a deeply rooted foundation of ethics and ancestry, intuition, relationships, and community while honoring your inner and outer cycles, you allow space for your full humanity in your magical practice. All aspects of you are welcome and needed, including your need to grieve, rest, experience pleasure, laugh, be curious, and be angry. It all holds value in the mundane and magical realms. Magic is an all-encompassing practice. May you feel the support within and around you as you craft your magic while we weave new worlds together.

# ᴀFTERWORD

I am sitting on wet earth with beloved Sycamore trees I've befriended. The sky is a haze with smoke from ongoing fires in Canada. My leg burns from a run-in with a patch of wood nettle, and I sense unrest within myself. Some parts of the forest feel strange and unfamiliar while simultaneously feeling like a part of me. The plants and bees show little concern for the smoke-filled sky as I consider putting on my KN95 mask. A family of deer congregates on the other side of the creek, speaking their language. Part of me resists understanding them. I am both out of place and at home. It is as if the lines between the magical and the mundane are weaving tighter within me, but navigating life with them requires moving in new ways. How do you walk in a living mystery?

My writing ritual for this book reminded me to root into my relationships with the more-than-human world, to stitch tighter the internal threads weaving the magical and the mundane in hopes of materializing something tangible. Sometimes the words flowed; sometimes I resisted them for fear of straying too far from the previously written ways to craft magic. My magical practice gave me a place to reorient when the feelings of strangeness rose too fast.

I don't think there will ever come a time when the unseen realms don't carry some element of strangeness—not in this human body. I've become increasingly comfortable with not knowing and taking guidance from otherworldly beings and nonlinear spaces. Remember to lean on your magical practice and the unseen relationships, even when unnamable mystery seeps in. Being with the

strangeness might be where our medicine lies in transient human bodies on an uncertain planet.

As you dance between the magical and mundane to craft your own magic and deepen more-than-human relationships, may this book offer guideposts along your sacred journey, reminding you that you're not alone in this. Weaving two worlds together, a foot in each, won't be neat and clean. Like the endless seedlings rooting in springtime to rise toward the sun, not all elements of your personal magical practice will survive. As it spirals in different directions, not every aspect will stay; *nor should it.* Crafting your own magic will require phases of death and shedding to make space for new pathways. You are responsible for making your own fertile ground. Hold tight; these transitional phases will create the life-giving compost for your next iteration.

A new phase will become known, whispering, "Come back. It's time to pick up where you left off, and remember how to weave worlds together." The magical invitations you receive might not always be your own, but they'll influence the whole nonetheless. Trusting these invitations and the sometimes unusual or unknown magic they may ask of you is a radical act—a deep and loving bow to the mystery.

My toes caked in dirt and my legs still itching from my forest romp, I'm back in another home. The TV is on in the background as my children watch their shows. Thoughts of tasks and to-dos enter my mind. The undercurrent of the mystery remains, with whispers to craft and collaborate magic never far. And I feel a sense of ease knowing that the unseen realms have stitched themselves tightly enough within me that they'll never leave. Maybe this is how new worlds come to be.

# ENDNOTES

## Chapter 1

1. The Pluralism Project, "Magick," December 12, 2023, https://pluralism.org/magick.

2. Etymonline, "Witch: Etymology of Witch by Etymonline," December 12, 2023, https://www.etymonline.com/word/witch.

3. "Curandero/Curandeiro: Encyclopedia.Com," December 10, 2023, https://www.encyclopedia.com/humanities/encyclopedias-almanacs-transcripts-and-maps/curanderocurandeiro.

4. Max Dashu, *Witches and Pagans: Women in Europe Folk Religion* (Richmond, CA: Veleda Press, 2016), 92.

5. "Indigenous Medicine and Traditional Healing: South African History Online," December 10, 2023, https://www.sahistory.org.za/article/indigenous-medicine-and-traditional-healing.

6. Dashu, *Witches and Pagans*, 93.

7. Dashu, *Witches and Pagans*, 94.

8. Dashu, *Witches and Pagans*, 97.

9. "Intersectionality," Anti-Racism Daily, December 26, 2022, https://antiracismdaily.com/glossary/intersectionality.

10. Regina Jackson and Saira Rao, *White Women: Everything You Already Know About Your Own Racism and How to Do Better* (New York: Penguin Books, 2022), 44.

11. Guy Ottewell, "EarthSky: The 5 Petals of Venus and Its 8-Year Cycle," EarthSky: Updates on Your Cosmos and World, January 23, 2023, https://earthsky.org/astronomy-essentials/five-petals-of-venus.

12. Erica Ekrem, "Transcript: Dr. BAYO AKOMOLAFE on Coming Alive to Other Senses /300," *For the Wild* podcast, January 23, 2023, https://forthewild.world/podcast-transcripts/dr-bayo-akomolafe-on-coming-alive-to-other-senses-300?rq=Bayo%20Akomolafe.

## Chapter 2

1.   Resmaa Menakem, *My Grandmother's Hands: Racialized Trauma and the Pathways to Mending Our Hearts and Bodies* (Las Vegas: Central Recovery Press, 2017), 39.

2.   Miami Nation of Indians of the State of Indiana, "The Miami Nation of Indiana," n.d., https://www.miamiindians.org/new-page-2.

3.   Barbara J. King, "Why You Should Think Twice about Those DNA-by-Mail Results," NPR, July 6, 2017, https://www.npr.org/sections/13.7/2017/07/06/535767665/why-you-should-think-twice-about-those-dna-by-mail-results; Ricketts, Rachel, *Do Better: Spiritual Activism for Fighting and Healing from White Supremacy* (New York, NY: Atria Books, 2021), 165.

4.   Jackson and Rao, *White Women*, 135.


## Chapter 3

1.   Benjet et al., "The Epidemiology of Traumatic Event Exposure Worldwide: Results from the World Mental Health Survey Consortium," *Psychological Medicine* 46, no. 2 (October 29, 2015): 327–43, https://doi.org/10.1017/s0033291715001981.

2.   Substance Abuse and Mental Health Services Administration, *Trauma-Informed Care in Behavioral Health Services*, Treatment Improved Protocol (TIP) Series 57, HHS Publication No. (SMA) 13–401, Rockville, MD: Substance Abuse and Mental Health Services Administration, 2014, https://www.ncbi.nlm.nih.gov/books/NBK207191/.

3.   Anne Llewellyn Barstow, *Witchcraze: A New History of the European Witch Hunts* (New York: HarperOne, 1994), 180.

4.   Haley Lewis, "Indigenous People Want Brands to Stop Selling Sage and Smudge Kits," HuffPost, December 3, 2018, https://www.huffpost.com/entry/indigenous-people-sage-and-smudge-kits_n_610874f5e4b0497e67026adb.

5.   Chevalier et al., "Earthing: Health Implications of Reconnecting the Human Body to the Earth's Surface Electrons," *Journal of Environmental and Public Health* 2012 (January 1, 2012): 1–8, https://doi.org/10.1155/2012/291541.

6.   Nayantara Dutta, "What It's Like to Be 'Mind Blind,'" *Time*, March 8, 2022, https://time.com/6155443/aphantasia-mind-blind/.


## Chapter 4

1.   "#22 Embodying the Unknown: Ellen Emmet," *Sounds of Sand* podcast, February 16, 2023, https://we.scienceandnonduality.com/podcasts/sounds-of-sand/episodes/2147862214.

2.   "Observe the Importance of a Mushroom's Mycelium in the Decomposition of Organic Matter," Brittanica, n.d., https://www.britannica.com/video/153021/role-fungi-decomposition-forest-litter.

3.  Paul G. Falkowski, "The Role of Phytoplankton Photosynthesis in Global Biogeochemical Cycles," *Photosynthesis Research* 39, no. 3 (March 1, 1994): 235–58, https://doi.org/10.1007/bf00014586.

## Chapter 5

1.  L. Reddy, M. W. Self, and P. Roelfsema, "How Does the Brain Learn to Link Things Together?," *Frontiers for Young Minds* 7 (January 9, 2020), https://doi.org/10.3389/frym.2019.00144.

2.  Gary Zabel, "Hunting Magic and Abbe Breuil," UMass Boston, n.d., https://www.faculty.umb.edu/gary_zabel/Courses/Phil%20281/Philosophy%20of%20Magic/My%20Documents/Hunting%20Magic%20and%20Abbe%20Breuil.htm.

3.  Peter Reuell, "Lessons in Learning," *Harvard Gazette*, September 4, 2019, https://news.harvard.edu/gazette/story/2019/09/study-shows-that-students-learn-more-when-taking-part-in-classrooms-that-employ-active-learning-strategies/.

## Chapter 6

1.  Alena Kuzub, "Human Exceptionalism Hinders Environmental Action, Northeastern Scientists Conclude," *Northeastern Global News*, July 24, 2023, https://news.northeastern.edu/2023/07/21/human-exceptionalism-environmental-action/.

2.  Philip Evich, "The Botany of Magnolias," Smithsonian Gardens, March 12, 2021, https://gardens.si.edu/learn/blog/the-botany-of-magnolias/.

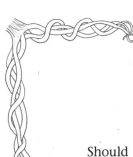

# ℞ESOURCES

Should you decide to expand your magical practice through learning from others, who you learn from will be unique to your location and ancestry. These teachers and their offerings are aimed at helping all uproot and heal from various systems of oppression that often interfere with our ability to form a deeply rooted and authentic magical practice.

### Recommended for all

Cultural Somatics Institute from Resmaa Menakem. : Find various courses and live trainings, including a free e-course. "Together let's set a course for healing historical and racialized trauma carried in the body and the soul." Learn more at https://courses.culturalsomaticsinstitute. com/collections.

### Recommended for Black, Brown, and/or Indigenous women and femmes of the global majority

Circle of Reclamation and Global Healing Festival with Embodied Black Girl, created by Thérèse Cator: "We center the thriving and liberation of BIPOC, specifically Black women and femmes and women of color. We believe that we all have a right to be well and we strive to close the gap that exists in wellness and mental health for our community." Learn more at embodiedblackgirl.com.

Rekindling the Fire of Our Sisterhood with Rematriation: "Rematriation offers the physical and virtual space for sisters to confer today's paramount concerns in a more natural way for Indigenous Women." Learn more at rematriation.com.

Decolonial Alchemy® with Dra. Rocío Rosales Meza: "For empathic, intuitive, visionary women of color and femmes of color ready to be keepers of possibility, not pain." Learn more at https://www.drrosalesmeza.com/offerings.

### Recommended for white and white-passing people of European descent

These are courses and intensives aimed at helping white and white-passing folks of European descent unlearn, heal, and make repairs. These are trainings that I have personally participated in, but there are many others. I encourage you to explore those too.

Embodied Solidarity with Thérèse Cator : An immersive experience designed to "uproot supremacy from your body and leadership" and to "uphold equity, justice, and liberation for all." Learn more at https://theresecator.com/offerings.

Decolonial Shadow Work® and other foundational teachings with Dra. Rocío Rosales Meza: Dra. Rocío's work "weaves decolonial teachings, Earth medicine, somatic work, energy work, and shadow work." Learn more at https://www.drrosalesmeza.com/offerings.

# BIBLIOGRAPHY

Adler, Margot. *Drawing Down the Moon: Witches, Druids, Goddess-Worshipers and Other Pagans in America*. New York: Penguin Group, 1986.

Akómoláfé, Báyò. *These Wilds Beyond Our Fences: Letters to My Daughter on Humanity's Search for Home*. Berkley, CA: North Atlantic Books, 2017.

Ambrose, Kala. *The Awakened Psychic: What You Need to Know to Develop Your Psychic Abilities*. Woodbury, MN: Llewellyn Publications, 2016.

Avalon, Annwyn. *The Way of the Water Priestess: Entering the World of Water Magic*. Newburyport, MA: Weiser Books, 2021.

Barkataki, Susanna. *How to Decolonize Your Yoga Practice* (blog). September 25, 2018. https://www.susannabarkataki.com/post/how-to-decolonize-your-yoga-practice.

Barstow, Anne Llewellyn. *Witchcraze: A New History of the European Witch Hunts*. New York: HarperOne, 1994.

Billington, Penny. *The Path of Druidry: Walking the Ancient Green Way*. Woodbury, MN: Llewellyn Publications, 2020.

Bird, Stephanie Rose. *African American Magick: A Modern Grimoire for the Natural Home*. Newburyport, MA: Red Wheel/Weiser, LLC, 2023.

brown, adrienne maree. *Emergent Strategy: Shaping Change, Changing Worlds*. Chica, CA: AK Press, 2017.

Condren, Mary. *The Serpent and the Goddess: Women, Religion, and Power in Celtic Ireland*. New York: HarperCollins, 1989.

Cowan, Tom. *Fire in the Head: Shamanism and the Celtic Spirit*. New York: HarperOne, 1993.

Cunningham, Scott and David Harrington. *Spell Crafts: Creating Magical Objects*. St. Paul, MN: Llewellyn Publications, 2003.

Dashu, Max. *Witches and Pagans: Women in Europe Folk Religion*. Richmond, CA: Veleda Press, 2016.

Estés, Clarissa Pinkola. *Women Who Run with the Wolves: Myths and Stories of the Wild Woman Archetype*. New York: Random House Publishing Group, 1995.

Estés, Clarissa Pinkola and Caroline Myss. *Intuition and the Mystical Life: Caroline Myss and Clarissa Pinkola Estés Bring Women's Wisdom to Light*. Louisville, CO: Sounds True, 2009.

Federici, Silvia. *Witches, Witch-Hunting, and Women.* Narrated by J. Lee Craig. Post Hypnotic Press Inc. Audible, 2021. Audiobook.

Fersko-Weiss, Henry. *Finding Peace at the End of Life: A Death Doula's Guide for Families and Caregivers.* Newburyport, MA: Red Wheel/Weiser, LLC, 2020.

Forest, Danu. *The Magical Year: Seasonal Celebrations to Honor Nature's Ever-Turning Wheel.* London: Watkins Media Limited, 2016.

Frost, Asha. *You Are the Medicine: 13 Moons of Indigenous Wisdom, Ancestral Connection, and Animal Spirit Guidance.* Carlsbad, CA: Hay House, Inc., 2022.

Gary, Gemma. *Silent as the Trees: Devonshire Witchcraft, Folklore and Magic.* London: Troy Books, 2017.

————— *Traditional Witchcraft: A Cornish Book of Ways.* London: Troy Books, 2008.

Geniusz, Mary Siisip. *Plants Have So Much to Give Us, All We Have to Do Is Ask: Anishinaabe Botanical Teachings.* Minneapolis, MN: University of Minnesota Press, 2015.

George, Demetra. *Mysteries of the Dark Moon: The Healing Power of the Dark Goddess.* New York: HarperOne–HarperCollins, 1992.

Gilbert, Elizabeth. *Big Magic: Creative Living beyond Fear.* New York: Riverhead Books, 2015.

Gottesdiener, Sarah Faith. *The Moon Book: Lunar Magic to Change Your Life.* New York: St. Martin's Essentials–St. Martin's Publishing Group, 2020.

Hanh, Thich Nhat. *The Heart of the Buddha's Teaching: Transforming Suffering into Peace, Joy, and Liberation.* New York: Broadway Books, 1998.

Harvey, Graham. *Animism: Respecting the Living World.* London: C. Hurst and Co., 2017.

Herstik, Gabriela. *Bewitching the Elements: A Guide to Empowering Yourself through Earth, Air, Fire, Water, and Spirit.* New York: TarcherPerigee, 2020.

hooks, bell. *Communion: The Female Search for Love.* New York: HarperCollins, 2002.

Jackson, Regina and Saira Rao. *White Women: Everything You Already Know About Your Own Racism and How to Do Better.* New York: Penguin Books, 2022.

Keppel, Anne-Marie. *Death Nesting: Ancient and Modern Death Doula Techniques, Mindfulness Practices and Herbal Care.* Self-published, 2019.

Kindred, Glennie. *Sacred Earth Celebrations.* Hampshire, United Kingdom: Permanent Publications, 2014.

Krawec, Patty. *Becoming Kin: An Indigenous Call to Unforgetting the Past and Reimagining Our Future.* Minneapolis, MN: Broadleaf Books, 2022.

Kynes, Sandra. *Llewellyn's Complete Book of Correspondences: A Comprehensive and Cross-Referenced Resource for Pagans and Wiccans.* Woodbury, MN: Llewellyn Publications, 2013.

Lahda, Alnoor. "Indigenous Languages and Encoded Quantum Physics: Tiokasin Ghosthorse." *Sounds of SAND.* Audio Podcast, November 23, 2022. https://we scienceandnonduality.com/podcasts/sounds-of-sand/episodes/2147826568.

Lee, Roberta / Nightwing. *Nightwing: Reflections of a Traditional Shaman.* Tempe, AZ: Bast Cat Enterprises, 2016.

———— *Sacred Wheel of Our Ancestors.* Tucson, AZ: FullCircle, 1993.

Lister, Lisa. *Witch: Unleashed. Untamed. Unapologetic.* Hay House UK. Narrated by Lisa Lister. Audible, 2017. Audiobook.

McDermott, Michael Reiley. "Embodying the Unknown: Ellen Emmet." *Sounds of SAND.* Podcast Audio, February 16, 2023. https://scienceandnonduality.com /podcasts/sounds-of-sand/episodes/2147862214.

McNamara, C. "What Are Values, Morals, and Ethics?" Management.org, January 29, 2022. https://management.org/blogs/business-ethics/2012/01/02/what-are-values-morals-and-ethics/.

Menakem, Resmaa. *My Grandmother's Hands: Racialized Trauma and the Pathways to Mending Our Hearts and Bodies.* Las Vegas, Nevada: Central Recovery Press, 2017.

Murphy-Hiscock, Arin. *Spellcrafting: Strengthen the Power of Your Craft by Creating and Casting Your Own Unique Spells.* Stoughton, MA: Adams Media–Simon and Schuster, Inc., 2020.

O'Brien, Lora. "Question—Irish Ancestry and Cultural Appropriation?" Lora O'Brien – Irish Author and Guide, November 25, 2020. https://loraobrien.ie/ances-try-cultural-appropriation/.

O'Driscoll, Dana. *A Magical Compendium of Eastern North American Trees: Ecology, History, Lore, and Divination.* The Druids Garden LLC, 2022.

Pearson, Nicholas. *Flower Essences from the Witch's Garden: Plant Spirits in Magickal Herbalism.* Rochester, VA: Destiny Books, 2022.

Pollack, Rachel. *Seventy-Eight Degrees of Wisdom: A Tarot Journey to Self-Awareness.* Newburyport, MA: Red Wheel/Weiser, LLC, 2019.

Ricketts, Rachel. *Do Better: Spiritual Activism for Fighting and Healing from White Supremacy.* New York: Atria Books–Simon and Schuster, Inc., 2021.

Saad, Layla F. *Me and White Supremacy: Combat Racism, Change the World, and Become a Good Ancestor.* Naperville, IL: Sourcebooks, 2020.

Salisbury, David. *Witchcraft Activism: A Toolkit for Magical Resistance.* Newburyport, MA: Red Wheel/Weiser, LLC, 2019.

Sentier, Elen. *Elen of the Ways: Following the Deer Trods, the Ancient Shamanism of Britain.* Hants, UK: Moon Books–John Hunt Publishing Ltd., 2013.

———— *Following the Deer Trods: A Practical Guide to Working with Elen of the Ways.* Hants, UK: Moon Books–John Hunt Publishing Ltd., 2014.

———— Starhawk. *The Spiral Dance: A Rebirth of the Ancient Religion of the Great Goddess.* San Francisco, CA: Harper and Row Publishers, 1979.

Strand, Sophie. *The Flowering Wand: Rewilding the Sacred Masculine.* Rochester, VT: Inner Traditions, 2022.

Thoma et al. "Preliminary Evidence: The Stress-Reducing Effect of Listening to Water Sounds Depends on Somatic Complaints." *Medicine,* February 2018, 97(8): e9851. https://www.ncbi.nlm.nih.gov/pmc/articles/PMC5842016/.

Valiente, Doreen. *An ABC of Witchcraft Past and Present.* New York: St. Martin's Press, 1973.

Van Der Hoeven, Joanna. *Pagan Portals—The Awen Alone: Walking the Path of the Solitary Druid*. Hants, UK: Moon Books, 2014.

Wachter, Aidan. *Six Ways: Approaches and Entries for Practical Magic*. Toronto, Canada: Red Temple Press, 2018.

———"What Is Rematriation?" Sogorea Te' Land Trust. November 11, 2023. https://sogoreate-landtrust.org/what-is-rematriation/.

Wild, Tara. "Pathways of Belonging and Courting the Sacred—Isla Macleod." *Dreaming the Ancestors*. Podcast Audio, 2023. https://podcasts.apple.com/cy/podcast/pathways-of-belonging-courting-the-sacred-isla-macleod/id1528394822?i=1000587410147.

Wilson, Sarah Durham. *Maiden to Mother: Unlocking Our Archetypal Journey into the Mature Feminine*. Louisville, CO: Sounds True, 2022.

Woodman, Marion. *Addiction to Perfection: The Still Unravished Bride*. Toronto, ON: Inner City Books, 1982.

Young, Ayana. "Sophie Strand on Myths as Maps." *For the Wild*. Podcast Audio, November 9, 2022. https://forthewild.world/podcast-transcripts/sophie-strand-on-myths-as-maps-312.

———. "Dr. Báyò Akómoláfé on Slowing Down in Urgent Times." *For the Wild*. Podcast Audio, January 22, 2020. https://forthewild.world/listen/bayo-akomolafe-on-slowing-down-in-urgent-times-155?rq=akomolafe.

———. "Dr. Báyò Akómoláfé on Coming Alive to Other Senses." *For the Wild*. Podcast Audio, August 17, 2022. https://forthewild.world/listen/dr-bayo-akomolafe-on-coming-alive-to-other-senses-300?rq=coming%20alive%20to%20other%20senses.

Young, Mimi. "Working with Correspondences as an Animist Witch." Ceremonie. March 18, 2023. https://shopceremonie.com/working-with-correspondences-as-an-animist-witch/.

# $\mathcal{A}$CKNOWLEDGMENTS

Thank you to my agent, Rita, who encouraged me to begin this process. Thank you, Anna, my editor, for trusting my vision, even as it changed, and for your gentle guidance. To my decolonial teachers, Thèrése Cator and Dra. Rocío Rosales Meza, thank you for being a part of my ongoing unlearning, healing, and repair that continues to restore my humanity. Appreciation and love to my sweet family, especially my supportive husband, who usually has more trust in me than I do, and my quickly growing children, who inspire me daily to continue on my path with integrity in hopes that I might leave this world more magical than it was when you both arrived. I am deeply grateful to my mother, siblings, and my father, in spirit, who support me even though they don't always understand me. Thank you for loving me as I am. To my chosen sisters, Sarah, Ashley, and Camden, who've supported me throughout my magical journey and in writing this book—thank you, and I love you. Thank you to my beloved human mentors and teachers, Robin and Sil. Your support and wisdom continue to shape me. Respect and reverence to the primordial Earth Mother, my guides, the tree spirits, and my ancestors who guide and support me—I am honored to be in community with you.

# ABOUT THE AUTHOR

**Cassie Uhl** (pronounced yule) is a magic-maker, death worker, intuitive energy worker, and the author and illustrator of several books and card decks. Her offerings are trauma-informed and rooted in animist and earth-based spiritual practices from her ancestral roots across northern Europe and her local environment. She is passionate about helping folks feel spiritually grounded and resourced in all seasons of life. She resides on Indigenous Myaamiaki land in so-called Indiana in the United States with her husband, twin children, and many beloved more-than-human friends. Learn more about Cassie, her work, and her offerings at **cassieuhl.com.**

## Hay House Titles of Related Interest

We hope you enjoyed this Hay House book. If you'd like to receive our online catalog featuring additional information on Hay House books and products, or if you'd like to find out more about the Hay Foundation, please contact:

Hay House LLC, P.O. Box 5100, Carlsbad, CA 92018-5100
(760) 431-7695 or (800) 654-5126
www.hayhouse.com® • www.hayfoundation.org

———

*Published in Australia by:*
Hay House Australia Publishing Pty Ltd
18/36 Ralph St., Alexandria NSW 2015
*Phone:* +61 (02) 9669 4299
www.hayhouse.com.au

*Published in the United Kingdom by:*
Hay House UK Ltd
The Sixth Floor, Watson House,
54 Baker Street, London W1U 7BU
*Phone:* +44 (0) 203 927 7290
www.hayhouse.co.uk

*Published in India by:*
Hay House Publishers (India) Pvt Ltd
Muskaan Complex, Plot No. 3,
B-2, Vasant Kunj, New Delhi 110 070
*Phone:* +91 11 41761620
www.hayhouse.co.in

———

## Let Your Soul Grow

Experience life-changing transformation—one video at a time—with guidance from the world's leading experts.

www.healyourlifeplus.com